L O V E

LIBERATION

&

THE LAW

LOVE

LIBERATION

& THE LAW

J. VERNON MCGEE

THE TEN COMMANDMENTS

THOMAS NELSON PUBLISHERS
Nashville • Atlanta • London • Vancouver

CONTENTS

WHY THE TEN COMMANDMENTS?

In New York City back in the old days Franklin D. Roosevelt Island was called Blackwell's Island. Prisoners were confined there, and a graveyard for criminals was there. If you should have walked through that cemetery, you would have seen on one of the tombstones a rather unusual epitaph that read like this:

> *Here lie the fragments of John Smith*
> *Who contradicted his Maker,*
> *Played football with the Ten Commandments,*
> *And departed this life at the age of thirty-five.*
> *His mother and wife weep for him.*
> *No one else does.*
> *May he rest in peace.*

Nobody can play football with the Ten Commandments and escape the judgment of God. Often the charge is made against those of us who preach the grace of God that we do not have a proper appreciation for the Law, especially the Ten Commandments—that we actually despise and reject it, teaching that because we're not saved by Law we can violate it at will and break it with impunity. On the contrary. Every preacher of the grace of God who has a true perspective of the nature of salvation by faith realizes the lofty character and majesty of the Law. He maintains a proper respect and reverence for it. And that man can say with the psalmist,

Oh, how love I thy law! It is my meditation all the day. (Psalm 119:97)

Now it might be well, as we begin, to inquire as to what the Law is, or to be specific, what are the Ten Commandments?

You can find this definition which has been given, and it is one of the oldest: "The Law is a transcript of the mind of God." Now may I say, that is a very defective definition. The Law is the expression of the mind of God *relative to what man ought to be,* but not of anything else. It is His will for man. And while the Law does express part of the nature and character of God, nowhere in the Law can you find mercy, grace, love and help, my beloved. These are not in the Law.

The Ten Commandments are the norm for human conduct. This God says very specifically in Micah 6:8:

He hath shown thee, O man, what is good; and what doth the LORD require of thee, but to do justly, and to love mercy, and to walk humbly with thy God?

May I say that this is Law undiluted and Law as God must give it. The Law, my beloved, comes down through human affairs today like a two-edged sword. In the last analysis, the Law lifts high those things which are right and boldly sets forth the things which are wrong that all men might see and read.

I remember, in studying a course in sociology in a state university, that the professor insisted there was no norm for right and wrong, that there was no way of distinguishing one from the other except by custom. May I say to you today that God has given His Law to let man know what is right and wrong. Stealing is wrong because God says it is wrong. Lying is wrong because God says it is wrong. And adultery is wrong because God says it is wrong, my beloved, and no man can change that.

Now another aspect of law we need to mention is that law never enforces itself. That was one of the reasons for the failure of the Eighteenth Amendment which prohibited the manufacture and sale of intoxicating liquors. A great many good people thought that after the Eighteenth Amendment was passed, prohibition would be established as a working law. But it had to be enforced—that was the problem, and it was finally repealed. Therefore we see that a lawgiver must also have power.

God, as the Lawgiver, has power. You see Him wrapping up even in natural laws of the material universe the penalties that go with breaking those laws. We call them laws of science or laws of nature today, and we see them in operation. They do not deviate. They are immutable. They are unchangeable.

I remember how saddened we were some time ago by a great tragedy in Southern California. Some precious little folk were killed by the falling of planes into a schoolyard in San Fernando. This came about because there is a law of nature in operation. We call it the law of gravity. And someone says, "Well, couldn't the God of love have suspended that law of gravity when those planes hit together and let them come down to earth like feathers?" Well, He could have, but my beloved, had He suspended the law of gravity, a greater tragedy would have taken place—all the residents in Los Angeles County would have floated out yonder into space! May I say to you, the law of gravitation is a law that never changes. It is immutable. It is unchangeable.

Somebody else says, "Well, why couldn't He have made a special dispensation just for those in the plane?" My beloved, one of the characteristics of any law is that it knows no persons. It plays no favorites. It has no pets. If it does, it is not law. And a judge who will rule otherwise is a crooked judge. He fails the high moral responsibility of his chosen field of service.

The picture of justice that Rome had and the world has adopted is personified as a woman. I have seen two statues of this at the entrance of the City Hall in Memphis, Tennessee. I've gone by there many times and looked at them there, one on each side of the entrance, identical statues of justice. They symbolize justice as a woman seated and blindfolded. She has balances in one hand, and at her side she is holding a sword. That is justice. And it has to be that way. It is represented as a woman because justice was to have the quality of tenderness in all decisions. It must not be judgment that comes from a harsh basis of hatred, wrath or bitterness. And she is blindfolded, since justice should be impartial, treating all alike—rich and poor, high and low. She holds in her left hand balances, because justice will weigh the evidence on both sides. And then, my friend, at her right side there is a sword, because when the law is violated there must be punishment. It is not law if it is otherwise.

In the moral realm you find the same thing, there is a penalty for breaking the law. God has made it that way. The writer to the Hebrews (chapter 10, verse 28) says, "He that despised Moses' law died without mercy. . . ." It had to be that way, or it wouldn't have been law. And then again in Leviticus 18:5, God says,

Ye shall therefore keep my statutes, and mine ordinances, which if a man do, he shall live in them: I am the LORD.

My friend, that means you cannot break them without paying the penalty. Laws must be enforced. Therefore He had to say in Deuteronomy 27:26: "Cursed be he who confirmeth not all the words of this law to do them. . . ."

We read in Numbers 15:32-36 about a man who went out to gather sticks on the Sabbath day, and in doing this he broke God's Law. He had despised the Word of the Lord and broken His commandment. That man was stoned to death. Yes, the Law is majestic. It plays no favorites, and it does not play down to man one whit!

Now there is another prevalent viewpoint concerning law that needs to be corrected today. It confounds law and grace, fusing them together into one system. That is confusion compounded in our country. A little booklet handed to me by someone from a new movement deals with essentials for salvation. It mentions three things you are to do, and one of them is, "Live life according to the Ten Commandments." Let me give you a quotation from this little book: "It is taught that the keeping of the Ten Commandments is not essential to salvation, that we are saved by faith alone. This is the destructive and devastating heresy that has invaded the church."

Oh, my friend, no one can ever stand up and say before God, "I kept the Law." God says the Law is perfect. You would have to be able to say that you obeyed it perfectly when you stand before God. To say that you believe in Christ and then try to keep the Law as a way of salvation— well, I say to you, anyone who will make a statement like that is either ignorant of the Law or is an egomaniac. When we turn to review the writings of the apostle Paul to both the Roman and Galatian believers, we can well understand why we have confusion in this land.

When you attempt to bring the Mosaic Law and grace together and fuse them together, law is robbed of its majesty and meaning, its design, its dignity and its purpose. And, my beloved, there is no love in law, there is no grace in law. When you try to blend the two together, grace is robbed of its goodness, its glow and its glory, its wonderment, its worthwhileness, its attractiveness and its desirability. And after you have brought them together, the claims of the Law are unanswered, and the sinner's needs are not met. The Law sets forth what man ought to be, and grace reveals what God is. Oh, I do want to show the majesty of the Law, its lofty position, and emphasize that no man dare trifle with its precepts or attempt to bring it down to his level and boast, "I've measured up to this." No man dare think today that he can be saved by keeping the Law.

Somebody asks, "Why then was the Law given?" Well, why were the Ten Commandments given? As we look at three reasons today, it is well to keep in mind this basic fact: The Law is good for the purpose for which it was designed, and it was never intended for any other purpose.

I heard of the country boy who came to a crossroads. One road sign there read, "Take this road to such and such (and it named the town where he wanted to go)," so he climbed up on the sign and sat down, waiting for it to take him there. Now that is a ridiculous story, but a great many people today are sitting on the Ten Commandments and saying, "We expect to go to heaven this way." You'd better take another vehicle, my friend. The Ten Commandments won't take you to heaven, but they will point you in the right direction.

The Law Reveals Who God Is

I want to mention now three reasons the Law was given. First of all, it was given to reveal who God is and the vast, yawning chasm between God and man. Paul writes in Galatians 4:21:

Tell me, ye that desire to be under the law, do ye not hear the law?

When you go back to Mt. Sinai, it is not a pretty sight, my beloved. Have you noticed, when God brought the children of Israel out of Egypt, how patient He was with them? For instance, think of that night when He delivered them and their firstborn because the blood had been applied to the doorpost. And by mighty power He took them across the Red Sea and led them to Mt. Sinai. And then He sent Moses down to say this to them: "Ye have seen . . . how I bore you on eagles' wings and brought you unto myself." He is asking, "Would you like to continue on eagles' wings, or would you like to have My Law?" And these people, with bold effrontery, audacious to say the least, said to God, "All that the LORD hath spoken we will do" (Exodus 19:8). They asked for it! And they got it, but they asked before they knew what it was. Their story is as sad and sordid as has ever been written. That nation, even today, is scattered throughout the world. And fundamentally the trouble in the Mideast today is because they broke God's Law. Yet here in our day there are people around us who say, "We have to get under Law to be saved."

Oh, my beloved, the giving of the Law was frightful. Will you notice the first thing God said when they asked for the Law? He said, "You go set bounds around Mt. Sinai, and tell them not to come any farther than that, lest they be killed."

And thou shalt set bounds unto the people round about, saying, Take heed to yourselves, that ye go not up into the mount, or touch the border of it; whosoever toucheth the mount shall be surely put to death. (Exodus 19:12)

And then we are told that God came down upon the mountain to give the Law:

And it came to pass on the third day in the morning, that there were thunders and lightnings, and a thick cloud upon the mount, and the voice of the trumpet exceedingly loud, so that all the people that were in the camp trembled. (Exodus 19:16)

My beloved, this was not a glorious, happy occasion—it was a frightening experience! Moses had no notion of leaving the impression that the giving of the Law was pleasant. It was terrifying!

Now will you notice this in Exodus 20:18, at the giving of the Law:

And all the people saw the thunderings, and the lightnings, and the noise of the trumpet, and the mountain smoking; and when the people saw it, they moved, and stood afar off.

They didn't come near God—they got away from Him, and they sent word back to Moses, "You speak to us, and we will listen; but don't let God speak to us lest we die!" And if people in our day really knew what the Law of God was, they would be afraid, my beloved, because you see, the Law would condemn all of us. What a picture is given here!

Then I call your attention to Psalm 19:7 where it says, "The law of the LORD is perfect." Because it is perfect it demands perfection. Our Lord Jesus Christ, when approached by a lawyer who asked Him which was the greatest commandment of the Law, took the Ten Commandments and summed them up in a few words. You see, the Ten Commandments are divided into two parts—

the first four are regarding man's relationship to God, and the last six concern man's relationship to man. So, when asked which is the greatest, the Lord Jesus said,

Thou shalt love the Lord, thy God, with all thy heart, and with all thy soul, and with all thy mind. This is the first and great commandment. And the second is like it, Thou shalt love thy neighbor as thyself. On these two commandments hang all the law and the prophets. (Matthew 22:37–40)

Do you want to come to God on that kind of basis? Are you prepared to tell God today that you do love Him, love Him every moment of the day and have loved Him with all your mind, your heart and your soul, that you have never loved or put anything ahead of Him? Are you prepared to say to God that you do love your neighbor as yourself? Unless you are, my beloved, stay away from the Ten Commandments as a means of *salvation*. They do not *save* you. They will condemn you.

"Weighed in the balances and found wanting" was the experience of a king in Daniel's day. And today, when the Ten Commandments are put on one side of the balances and you or I step on the other, we will fall short. We will have been found wanting, my friend. And there is no use for you to look at me and say, "I'm so much better than you." That won't help you a bit. May I say to you, the man on top of Mt. Whitney may be a great deal higher than the man on top of an ant hill, but both of them are a long, long way from heaven. There's really not much difference. And today we have come short of the glory of God. You may have a Mt. Whitney type of character and be able to boast of your life, but in God's sight you stand condemned by the Law. The Law reveals who God is, and it reveals how far man and God are apart.

The Law Reveals Who Man Is

The second thing that the Law does is to reveal who man is and that he is unable to bridge the gap between himself and God in his own strength. This is the way the Scripture reads in Romans 3:19, 20:

Now we know that whatever things the law saith, it saith to them who are under the law, that every mouth may be stopped, and all the world may become . . .

Become what? Saved? No—

. . . become guilty before God. Therefore, by the deeds of the law there shall no flesh be justified in his sight; for by the law is the knowledge of sin.

The Law reveals to man who he is. It was never given to save us, you see. It was given to reveal *who we are*.

Remember the fairy story in which the bad queen stood before the mirror and said,

> *Mirror, mirror on the wall,*
> *Who's the fairest of them all?*

Well, she wasn't the fairest, and the mirror told her she wasn't. My beloved, the Law is a mirror, the Epistle of James calls it a mirror:

For if any be a hearer of the word, and not a doer, he is like a man beholding his natural face in a mirror; for he beholdeth himself, and goeth his way, and immediately forgetteth what manner of man he was. (James 1:23, 24)

You see, the Law is a mirror revealing the sin in our hearts. But in no way does it remove the sin. You go to a mirror to see the spot on your face, but the mirror won't take it off. You have to turn to something else. The Law is a revealer, showing us who we are.

There is an old parable about an angel who appeared to a man as he was walking down the road and walked along with him. In the distance, they saw a man who was coming toward them, and the angel said, "You see that man yonder?"

"Yes, he's my neighbor."

"Well, that man you see is sly, he's cunning, he lies. He is not to be trusted."

Hearing that made this fellow feel pretty good. I wonder if it makes us feel good to hear something bad about somebody else. This man felt very comfortable and superior when the angel said that about his neighbor. As they continued walking and talking about him, they were approaching this neighbor. Finally, when they came right up to him, suddenly the man realized that it was not his neighbor after all. They had been walking toward a mirror all the time!

May I say that the Word of God as a mirror lets us see our lives. Also the Law is a searchlight put down on us, and it reveals the sin in our hearts, but in no way does it remove that sin, my beloved. The Law cannot save us. God tells us in the New Testament what the Law cannot do:

For what the law could not do, in that it was weak through the flesh, God sending his own Son, in the likeness of sinful flesh and for sin, condemned sin in the flesh. (Romans 8:3)

It just couldn't save us. While it does reveal our sin, it does not make us sinners. The mirror never makes a spot on your face. The mirror only reveals that spot to you. And that is what Paul wrote in Galatians 4:9:

But now, after ye have known God, or rather are known by God, how turn ye again to the weak and beggarly elements, unto which ye desire again to be in bondage?

Why return to the bondage of the Law? The Law reveals and it condemns; but the Law cannot save. The apostle James mentioned the Law's bondage:

For whosoever shall keep the whole law, and yet offend in one point, he is guilty of all. (James 2:10)

Sometimes we pride ourselves on some particular accomplishment. I know of a man who prides himself on his truthfulness. He says that he never in his life has told a lie nor has he misrepresented anything. That is a very fine reputation to have. But you see, he forgets about some of the other laws. James said that if a man kept all the Law yet broke just one part of it, he would be a lawbreaker. One little hole in the dam will let all the water out. The rest of the dam may be good. There may be one little hole in the radiator of your automobile and the rest of it may be in perfect condition, but the water will run out, and you'll come to a steaming stop. If we stumble or offend the Law even in one part, we are guilty of all. The Law reveals who man is.

The Law Leads Us to Christ

Finally, the Law was given to bring a person to Christ. Did you know this is the basic reason that God gave the Law? The Bible makes this very clear by using the illustration of a schoolmaster:

Wherefore, the law was our schoolmaster to bring us unto Christ, that we might be justified by faith. But after faith is come, we are no longer under a schoolmaster. (Galatians 3:24, 25)

The Law was given in order that we might see who God is and that we might see ourselves and also see the great chasm between us that we cannot bridge. The Law was a slave, if you please, for that was what the schoolmaster was who is spoken of here.

The word "schoolmaster" is the Greek *paidagogos*, and it doesn't mean school teacher. *Schoolmaster* is a good word, but it meant something quite different back in the days of Paul. It meant a servant or a slave who was part of a Roman household. Half of the Roman Empire was slave. Of a population numbering 120 million, 60 million were slaves. In the homes of the patricians, the members of the Praetorian Guard, and the rich in the Roman Empire, were slaves who cared for the children. When a child was born into such a home, he was put in the custody of a servant or a slave who actually raised him. He put clean clothes on him, bathed him, blew his nose when it was necessary, and paddled him when he needed it. When the little one grew to a certain age and was to start to school, this servant was the one who got him up in the morning, dressed him, and took him to school. (That is where the slave got the name of *paidagogos. Paid* has to do with the feet—and we get our word *pedal* from it; *agogos* means "to lead.") It means that he takes the little one by the hand, leads him to school, and turns him over to the school teacher. This slave was not capable of teaching him beyond a certain age, so he took him to school.

Now what Paul is saying here is that the Law is our *paidagogos.* In effect the Law says, "Little fellow, I can't do any more for you. I now want to take you by the hand and bring you to the cross of Christ. You are lost. You need a Savior." The purpose of the Law is to bring men to Christ—not to give us an expanded chest so we can walk around claiming we keep the Law. You *know* you don't keep the Law; all you have to do is examine your own heart to know that. When you see your hopeless, helpless condition, the Law then becomes the one who takes you by the hand and brings you to Christ. Christ is the One who kept the Law, and because He died on the cross, paying the penalty for your sin, it is possible for a holy God to accept you without lowering His standard. The penalty is paid, and now He can receive you, a vile sinner, a lawbreaker, a transgressor, and bring you into the presence of God.

Oh, my friend, let the Law fulfill its purpose in your life. And if it does, it will bring you to Christ, bring you to the Savior and turn you over to Him. I don't know about you, but I don't want to come to God by Law. If I do, I am condemned. I am lost forever. But I come to Calvary and find forgiveness there and pardon and the love of God. He has said to even me and to you, "Come . . . come . . . come."

When I was a student in seminary, I was driving from

Atlanta, Georgia to Nashville, Tennessee. I went through Chattanooga and came up over Lookout Mountain on that old highway in those days. It was during the Depression. The highway was very narrow, and as I started down the mountain on the other side I saw ahead of me an old, broken-down Model-T truck. It was occupied by what we call in the South a "cropper," that is, a share-cropper. Poor fellow. He had gotten out of the truck. I could see his brow was furrowed—he was worried, looking down at the engine—and his wife was standing there. I had to just crawl to get around them, and as I did, I heard somebody talking. Looking over, I saw a little girl a ragged little girl about six years old, sitting in the seat. She had in her arms a dolly, and I have never seen a dolly that was as battered as that dolly. One of its arms was gone. It didn't have a stitch of clothing on it, and its china head was practically broken off—just parts of it jutting up. But I never saw such affection bestowed by anyone. That little girl was oblivious to what was going on, the fact that the truck was broken down or that anybody was seeing her. She just held that little broken dolly in her arms and poured out her little mother's heart, telling it how much she loved it. And I thought as I left there that day and rode on alone, *What love, to love a thing like that.*

But I want to tell you, friend, I know a love greater than that. May I say that when we were dead in trespasses and sins, we were much more unattractive than that little dolly, but God put His mighty arms around us and said, "I love you, I love you." Even while we were dead in sins, God loved us! Christ died for the ungodly!

For God so loved the world, that he gave his only begotten Son, that whosoever believeth in him

should not perish, but have everlasting life. (John 3:16)

"God so loved . . . that he gave. . . ." And there at Calvary was His mighty heart of love poured out.

A little broken dolly receiving all that love and affection could not respond. What a tragedy. And today God loves you the same way, and if you have never responded, what a tragedy!

CHAPTER 1

NO OTHER GODS
The First Commandment

I am the LORD thy God, who have brought thee out of the land of Egypt, out of the house of bondage. Thou shalt have no other gods before me. (Exodus 20:2,3)

"I am the LORD thy God . . ." is literally, "I am Jehovah thy God." The name *Jehovah* is made up of three Hebrew words meaning, "He who will be, He who is, He who was."

Our little minds have difficulty in comprehending a Being who never had a beginning and will never have an end. We can think back to creation, and He is there. We try to think back billions and trillions of years, and He comes out of eternity to meet us.

This identification of Himself brings us into the presence of the eternal Sovereign of the universe, our own Creator who loves us!

Now note His first commandment: "Thou shalt have no other gods before me." Certainly it is a reasonable request when we learn who He is.

Oh, my friend, do you and I put Him first? Or are we engaged in the very things that the world is engaged in— and for which God intends to judge them? Well, how then can we expect that we shall escape the judgment of God? If you are in Christ, "seek those things which are above," and you will not find yourself involved in the things of the world. God's Word says, "Thou shalt have no other gods before me."

You see, the people of Israel were in a land of idolatry when they lived in Egypt, and they lived in an age of idolatry. Early on, man's sin was not atheism; his sin was polytheism. He worshiped many gods. For example, at the Tower of Babel men built a ziggurat, a tower. On the top of this tower they offered sacrifices, apparently to the sun—the sun and the planets were some of the first objects men worshiped when they turned away from God. After the Flood, they certainly were not worshiping thunder and lightning because those were connected with the Flood, and they feared them. Instead they worshiped the sun, the creation rather than the Creator. It was for the polytheist that God said, "Thou shalt have no other gods before me."

It was not until the time of David that atheism came in. Earlier than that, men were too close to the mooring mast of revelation to be atheists. The revelation of God was still in their memory, and no one was denying the existence of God.

Atheism Corrupts the World

Then, perhaps a millennium before Christ, the atheist begins to appear on the scene. We have a glimpse of him in Psalm 10:4, which says, "The wicked, through the pride of his countenance, will not seek after God; God is not in all his thoughts." A better translation of this is, "All his thoughts are, 'There is no God!'" And he exhibits the very depth of human depravity.

When the atheists began to appear during the time of David, they were called fools:

The fool hath said in his heart, There is no God. They are corrupt, they have done abominable works, there is none that doeth good. (Psalm 14:1)

The Hebrew word for "fool" in this verse is *nabal*. This may ring a bell in your thinking, because there was a man by the name of Nabal who was married to a lovely woman by the name of Abigail. His story is told in 1 Samuel 25. His name certainly characterized him accurately. He acted a fool. The word *nabal* may be translated as simple, silly, simpleton, fool, or madman.

Knowing what we do about the universe today, only a madman would say that there is no God. Man has found that the universe works more accurately than any clock or watch he has been able to make. And there is no watch walking around that "just happened"—some watchmaker made it. The universe that is timed more accurately than a watch tells us that there is a universe Maker. The *fool* has said in his heart that there is no God.

There are many people with Ph.D.s who are teaching in our universities today. Many of them are atheists. I want to say this carefully: The lowest that a man can sink in human depravity is to be an atheist. That is what the Word of God says. If you do not believe there is a God, you are a fool. You do not have any real sense. Having a high I.Q. is not enough.

I used to teach with a man who had a Ph.D., and he didn't have sense enough to get out of the rain. I played golf with him one day when it began to rain. He looked at me and asked, "What shall we do?" He was really asking for information! What would any sensible person do when it starts pouring down rain?

I said to him, "I think we had better get in out of the rain!" Even I knew that, but he didn't seem to know. So you see, a scholastic degree doesn't prove a man's

intelligence! "They are corrupt, they have done abominable works, there is none that doeth good."

I believe you will find that most atheists are also great
sinners. Gross immorality is generally one of their characteristics. A man who mixes with the college set told
me, "It is amazing the number of Ph.D.s who claim to
be atheists and who are living in gross immorality. And
some of them actually live in filth—and I mean material,
physical filth."

> **The LORD looked down from heaven upon the chil-
> dren of men, to see if there were any that did under-
> stand, and seek God.** (Psalm 14:2)

And what did He find?

> **They are all gone aside, they are all together become
> filthy; there is none that doeth good, no, not one.**
> (Psalm 14:3)

This verse is repeated in Romans 3:12, "They are all gone
out of the way, they are together become unprofitable;
there is none that doeth good, no, not one." Paul is speaking not only about atheists here; he is speaking about
everyone. This is a picture of you and me, friend. I am
not an atheist, and I don't imagine you are, but we are
sinners. We do not do "good." The condition of man is
corrupt, and these verses tell us the depths to which
mankind can go.

Always a Witness

You see, there is a natural revelation of God, as Paul
explains in Romans 1:18,19:

For the wrath of God is revealed from heaven against all ungodliness and unrighteousness of men, who hold the truth in unrighteousness, because that which may be known of God is manifest in them; for God hath shown it unto them.

The "wrath of God is revealed." Actually, if you want to know what salvation really is, you have to know how bad sin is. Stifler says, "Sin is the measure of salvation." The wrath of God is God's feeling, not His punishment of sin. It is His holy anger. Wrath is the antithesis of righteousness, and it is used here as a correlative.

"The wrath of God is being revealed" is God's answer to those who assert that the Old Testament presents a God of wrath, while the New Testament presents a God of love. There is a continuous revelation not only of God's love but of the wrath of God in both the Old Testament and the New Testament. It is revealed in our contemporary society. There is God's constant and insistent displeasure with evil. He changes not. God is merciful, not because He is lenient with the sinner but because Christ died for our sins.

The suffering and death of Christ Jesus has not changed God's attitude toward sin, but it has made it possible for God to accept the sinner. The sinner must have either the righteousness or the wrath of God. Both are revealed from heaven. And you can see it on every hand. If you want to know how bad sin is, look at the cases of venereal diseases today. You don't get by with sin, my friend. I won't give personal illustrations, but I have been a pastor long enough to see again and again the judgment of God upon sin. It is revealed from heaven. Also there will be a final judgment when the small and great stand before God (Revelation 20:11–15).

"The wrath of God is . . . against all ungodliness"—

ungodliness is that which is against God. It is that which denies the character of God. Oh, the irreligiousness of today! There are multitudes of people who disregard the very existence of God. That is the state of a person's soul. That is sin.

While ungodliness is against God, unrighteousness is against man. What does it mean? It is the denial of the rule of God. It is the action of the soul. That man who gets drunk, goes out on the freeway, breaks the traffic laws and kills someone—that man is unrighteous. He is sinning against man. Another example is the man who is dishonest in his business dealings. God hates man's unrighteousness, and He will judge it.

God is angry at people who hold the truth in unrighteousness—literally it means to hold down, suppress the truth in unrighteousness. The wrath of God is revealed against folk who do this.

For the invisible things of him from the creation of the world are clearly seen, being understood by the things that are made, even his eternal power and Godhead, so that they are without excuse. (Romans 1:20)

There is an original revelation from God. This universe in which you and I live tells two things about God: His person and His power. This has been clearly seen from the time the world was created.

How can invisible things be seen? Paul makes this a paradox purposely to impress upon his readers that the "dim light of nature" is a man-made falsehood. Creation is a clear light of revelation. It is the primary revelation. The psalmist said,

When I consider thy heavens, the work of thy fingers, the moon and the stars, which thou hast ordained. (Psalm 8:3)

Again we read in Psalm 19:1,

The heavens declare the glory of God; and the firmament sheweth his handiwork.

Romans 1:20 speaks of "His eternal power and Godhead," that is, His eternal power and deity, power and Person. Creation reveals the unchangeable power and existence of God. And in Acts 14:17 we read, ". . . he left not himself without witness, in that he did good, and gave us rain from heaven, and fruitful seasons, filling our hearts with food and gladness."

Dr. James Denny writes, "There is that within man which so catches the meaning of all that is without, as to issue in an instinctive knowledge of God." I think the most ridiculous position man can hold is that of atheism. It is illogical and senseless. Creation so clearly reveals God that man is without excuse. The historical basis of man's sin did not come about through ignorance. It was willful rebellion in the presence of clear light.

Getting to Know Him

Many pagan folk recognize that behind their idolatry is a living and true God. They know nothing about Him, and they do not know how to approach Him. But they have traditions that back in the dim and distant past their ancestors did worship Him.

When Paul was in Athens, his spirit was stirred, seeing the whole city given over to idolatry. Athens was the cultural center of the world. In fact, when one thinks of Athens, one thinks about culture. Yet it was a city filled with idolatry.

And so Paul began to speak out:

Therefore disputed he [Paul] in the synagogue with the Jews, and with the devout persons, and in the market place daily with them that met with him. Then certain philosophers of the Epicureans, and of the Stoics, encountered him. . . . And they took him, and brought him unto Areopagus, saying, May we know what this new doctrine, of which thou speakest, is? For thou bringest certain strange things to our ears. We would know, therefore, what these things mean. (For all the Athenians and strangers who were there spent their time in nothing else, but either to tell, or to hear some new thing.) (Acts 17:17–21)

The Areopagus is a very peculiar formation of rock on top of which the Parthenon and the buildings connected with it stand. Frankly, it is a very lovely setting, beautiful buildings and beautiful statues, but a city wholly given over to idolatry. The Areopagus was situated up from the market place of the city, and Paul was brought there to speak. Probably every preacher who visits there reads Paul's sermon from the top of Mars' Hill. When I was there another preacher began to read it, and since I didn't like the way he was doing it, I went way over to the other side of the rock. I sat with my Bible and read it silently. It was a thrilling experience.

Now going back to the first century, these Greek philosophers say to him, "May we know what this new doctrine, of which thou speakest, is?" They want to know more about it. They are completely in the dark. They are worse off than the Galatians or the people in Philippi and Thessalonica. Why? Because they think they know something. The very hardest people in the world to reach with the Word of God and the gospel of Christ are church members because they think they don't need it. They think the gospel is for the man on skid row and for some of their friends. Some church members can be mean and sinful and yet not recognize they really need a Savior, not only to save them from sin, but also to make their lives count for God.

Now notice that everybody was spending their time trying to tell or hear something new. In this same way America is going to seed today. Have you ever listened to the talk shows? They are boring to tears. Everyone is trying to come up with something new. Each one is trying to say something novel. They try so hard to say something smart and sophisticated, yet it is the same old story. Athens tried the same thing. There must have been a bunch of loafers back in Athens. They didn't work— they didn't do anything. They just talked, propounding new theories and new ideas.

The human family seems to reach that place of sophistication. They think they know something when they don't. They don't know the most important fact in the whole universe.

Then Paul stood in the midst of Mars' Hill, and said, Ye men of Athens, I perceive that in all things ye are very religious. (Acts 17:22)

He was saying that he perceived they were in all things *too* religious. The Athenians were very religious. Athens was filled with idols. There was no end to the pantheon of gods which the Athenians and the Greeks had. There were gods small and gods great—they had a god for practically everything. That is what Paul is saying. They were too religious.

I sometimes hear people ask, "Why should we send missionaries to foreign countries? Those people have their own religion." I suppose when Paul went down to Athens, somebody said, "Why are you going down there? They have religion." I am sure Paul would have answered, "That's their problem; they have too much religion."

A preacher friend of mine said many years ago, "When I came to Christ, I lost my religion." There are a great many folk in our churches today who need to lose their religion so they can find Christ. That is the great problem. Some folk say, "People are too bad to be saved." The real problem is that people are too good to be saved. They think they are religious and worthy and good. My friend, we are to take the gospel of Christ to all because all people are lost without Christ, which is the reason Paul went to Athens. The Athenians needed to hear the message of the gospel.

After Paul makes the observation that the Athenians are too religious, he continues,

For as I passed by, and beheld your devotions, I found an altar with this inscription, TO THE UNKNOWN GOD. Whom, therefore, ye ignorantly worship, him declare I unto you. (Acts 17:23)

Notice that he said, "I beheld your devotions." He saw their objects of worship. He noted their altars and their idols and their temples. In fact, that very beautiful temple called the Parthenon was a temple built to Athena, the virgin goddess of the Athenians. There were idols all around. Paul said, "I observed all of this, and amidst the idols I found an altar inscribed to the unknown god."

Whatever the reason for there being an altar to the

unknown god, Paul used it as a springboard for his message. He said he wanted to talk to them about this unknown god. He said he wanted to tell them about the God whom they did not know.

Creator

Now the Athenians thought they knew everything. This crowd of philosophers met in Athens and talked back and forth, as philosophers do on college campuses today. And now Paul begins to talk to them about the God they do not know. Who is He? Well, first of all, He is the God of creation.

> **God who made the world and all things in it, seeing that he is Lord of heaven and earth, dwelleth not in temples made with hands, neither is worshiped with men's hands, as though he needed any thing, seeing he giveth to all life, and breath, and all things; and hath made of one blood all nations of men to dwell on all the face of the earth, and hath determined the times before appointed, and the bounds of their habitation.** (Acts 17:24–26)

God had made very clear all the way through the Old Testament—even when He gave Israel the pattern for the tabernacle and the temple—that He did not dwell in one geographical spot. Solomon acknowledged this in his prayer at the dedication of the temple: "But will God indeed dwell on the earth? Behold, the heaven and heaven of heavens cannot contain thee; how much less this house that I have built!" (1 Kings 8:27). These men in the Old Testament recognized that God the Creator, the living God, could not live in a building that had been made by man. Man lives in a universe that God has made.

Why does man get the idea that he can build a building for God to live in?

Now, in a masterful stroke, Paul tells them, "God doesn't need anything from you. You built an altar to Him; you bring offerings to feed Him." They wanted this unknown God to know that they were thinking of Him. But now Paul says, "God doesn't need anything from you! God is on the giving end. He gives you life. He gives you your breath. He has given you the sun, the moon, and the stars. He has given you all things." These Athenians worshiped the sun. They said that Apollo came dragging his chariot across the sky every day. Paul says that the sun is something that God has made, and it is a gift for you. The Creator is the living God. He is the One who has given you everything. By the way, He gives you salvation also. He not only gives you physical things but also gives you spiritual gifts.

"And hath made of one blood . . . ." So much has been made of this phrase that I think we need to dissipate any wrong notions here. A better translation is, "He made from one every nation of mankind." God has made one humanity. This verse is not talking about brotherhood. The only brotherhood which Scripture knows is the brotherhood of those who are in Christ Jesus. Perhaps I should amend that by saying there is also a brotherhood of sin. We all are sinners.

Paul's statement that God "hath determined the times before appointed, and the bounds of their habitation" is fascinating. Not only is He the God who created the universe and who created human beings, but it is interesting to note that He also put them in certain geographical locations.

My doctor is a cancer specialist and he has told me to stay out of the sun here in California because I am a blonde. There seems to be even a medical reason why

God put the darker races where the sun shines and put the light-skinned races up north where there is not so much sun. So some of us who are blonde and light-skinned need to be very careful about too much exposure to the sun. God is the One who has determined the geographical locations for His creatures. I guess some of my ancestors should have stayed where they belonged. Maybe I'm kind of out of place here in California, but I'm glad to be here and I try to be careful about protecting myself from too much sunshine.

God has put nations in certain places. It is interesting that the thing which has produced wars of the past is that nations don't want to stay where they belong. They want someone else's territory. That has been the ultimate cause for every war that has ever been fought.

Now man is not necessarily looking for the living and true God, but he is on a search.

That they should seek the Lord, if perhaps they might feel after him, and find him, though he is not far from every one of us; for in him we live, and move, and have our being; as certain also of your own poets have said, For we are also his offspring. (Acts 17:27, 28)

This phrase "feel after him" has the idea of groping after Him. Man is not really searching for the living and true God, but he is searching for a god. He is willing to put up an idol and worship it.

Note that Paul does not call them sons of God but the offspring of God. He is referring to creation and the relationship to God through creation. And by the way, this is not pantheism which he is stating here. He is not saying that everything is God. He says that in God "we live, and move, and have our being," but God is beyond this created universe.

Paul quotes to them from their own poets. One of the poets he quoted was Arastus who lived about 270 B.C. He was a Stoic from Cilicia. He began a poem with an invocation to Zeus in which he said that "we too are his offspring." Cleanthes was another poet who lived about 300 B.C. He also wrote a hymn to Zeus and speaks of the fact that "we are his offspring." Paul means, of course, that we are God's creatures.

Redeemer

Having shown that God is the Creator, Paul now presents Him as the Redeemer.

> **Forasmuch, then, as we are the offspring of God, we ought not to think that the Godhead is like gold, or silver, or stone, carved by art and man's device. And the times of this ignorance God overlooked, but now commandeth all men everywhere to repent.** (Acts 17:29, 30)

There was a time when God shut His eyes to paganism. Now light has come into the world. God asks men everywhere to turn to Him. Light creates responsibility. Now God is commanding all men everywhere to repent.

Judge

Paul has presented God as the Creator in His past work. He shows God as the Redeemer in His present work. Now he shows God as the Judge in His future work:

> **Because he hath appointed a day, in which he will judge the world in righteousness by that man whom**

he hath ordained; concerning which he hath given assurance unto all men, in that he hath raised him from the dead. (Acts 17:31)

When God judges, it will be right. Judgment will be through a Judge who has nail-pierced hands, the One who has been raised from the dead. Paul always presents the resurrection of Jesus Christ. The resurrection of Jesus Christ from the dead is a declaration to all men. It is by this that God assures there will be a judgment.

And when they heard of the resurrection of the dead, some mocked; and others said, We will hear thee again of this matter. So Paul departed from among them. (Acts 17:32, 33)

Do you know why they mocked? Because Platonism denied the resurrection of the dead. That was one of the marks of Platonism. It denied the physical resurrection. When you hear people today talking about a *spiritual* resurrection but denying the *physical* resurrection, you are hearing platonic philosophy rather than scriptural teaching. Because Paul taught the physical resurrection from the dead, when these Platonists heard of the resurrection of the dead they mocked. And so Paul departed.

Now some critics have said that Paul failed at Athens. He didn't fail, friend. There will always be those who mock at the gospel. But there will also be those who believe: "Nevertheless, certain men joined him, and believed . . ." (Acts 17:34). And where the Word of God is preached, there will be those who will listen and believe.

CHAPTER 2

IDOLATRY EXPOSED
The Second Commandment

Thou shalt not make unto thee any carved image, or any likeness of anything that is in heaven above, or that is in the earth beneath, or that is in the water under the earth. (Exodus 20:4)

When I drove to my office this morning there were a great many people on their way to work. Many of them were professional men and business executives. One man went by me in a Cadillac. He didn't see me or anyone else because he was in such a hurry. I don't know why he was hurrying, but I can guess. We see pictures of people in other lands going to heathen temples and worshiping there, and we feel sorry for them in the darkness of their idolatry. But I suspect that the fellow in the Cadillac was also in darkness, that he was on his way to worship his idol and to bow before it—that his idol was the almighty dollar, and he was rushing to work to see how many he could make.

Again and again in Old Testament times the prophets warned against the sin of idolatry, saying that because of it the whole nation of Israel would go down. The prophet Micah describes the specific sins of the people:

Woe to them that devise iniquity, and work evil upon their beds! When the morning is light, they practice it, because it is in the power of their hand. (Micah 2:1)

Judgment came upon these people because they had gone into unbridled covetousness and idolatry with all that implies. I have had some experience with folk like this. A wife complained to me bitterly that when her husband comes home, he doesn't leave his work in the office but brings it with him. And when he goes to bed at night, he lies there conniving what he will do the next day. No wonder the wife was contemplating divorce. To some people, their bank book is their god. But there are many other gods being worshiped in our day, as we shall see.

What Is Idolatry?

Actually, anything that takes first place in your heart is your idol. Anything that you give yourself to, especially in abandonment, becomes your "god." Many people who would deny worshiping Bacchus, the cloven-hoofed Greek and Roman god of wine and revelry of long ago, worship the bottle just the same. There are millions of alcoholics in our country right now. The liquor interests like to tell us about how much of the tax burden they carry, when actually they do not pay a fraction of the bill for the casualties they cause by their product. Whether or not these folk recognize it, they do worship the god Bacchus.

Or they may be worshiping Aphrodite; that is, the goddess of sex. In Colossians 3:5 we're instructed to "Mortify [put in the place of death], therefore, your members which are upon the earth: fornication [sexual immorality], uncleanness [includes thoughts, gestures, jokes], inordinate affection [uncontrolled lust], evil desire, and covetousness (which is idolatry)." Covetousness is when we always must have more. And that is idolatry.

Idolatry in that day represented gross immorality, and the wages of harlots ran the "high places" which the prophets warned against. Prostitution was the source of funds for their religion since sex was associated with idolatry. We find that the same thing is true today in the occult and in Satan worship. I think there is a connection between the occult of today and the idolatry of Micah's day. Sex plays a very prominent part in both of them.

Sexual sin and idolatry seem to go together. They destroy the home and destroy the sweet and tender relationship between a man and a woman in marriage. When sex is kept within the marriage relationship, it can become the sweetest and most precious thing on earth. When a nation moves sex out of that context and encourages illicit sex in the name of religion or "new morality," it is evidence of the fact that the nation is in decline and is actually on its way out.

Thou shalt not bow down thyself to them, nor serve them; for I, the LORD thy God, am a jealous God, visiting the iniquity of the fathers upon the children unto the third and fourth generation of them that hate me; and showing mercy unto thousands of them that love me, and keep my commandments. (Exodus 20:5, 6)

These verses have presented a problem to many people. Is God being unfair? Will He punish the children of sinning parents? Dr. G. Campbell Morgan gives a fine interpretation of this:

To pass on to children a wrong conception of God . . . is the most awful thing a man can do. . . . When a man puts something, as the object of his worship, in the place of God, he passes on the same practice to his offspring. What a terrible heritage he is thus handing down to the child!

But notice the gracious promise standing side by side with the warning: . . . "Showing mercy unto a thousand generations of them that love Me, and keep My commandments." . . . Here is a remarkable comparison—God visits the iniquity to the third and fourth generation; but He shows mercy unto the thousandth generation! If a man will commit to his posterity a worship which is true, strong, whole-hearted, and pure, and will sweep away all that interferes between himself and God, he is more likely to influence for good the thousandth generation that follows him than a man of the opposite character is to touch that generation with evil. . . . Whenever a man stops short of that face-to-face worship of the Eternal God, he is working ruin to his own character, because he is breaking the commandment of God. (Morgan, *The Ten Commandments*, pp. 34, 35)

Jeremiah Deals with It

In the prophecy of Jeremiah, God condemns the people of Israel on two scores: they have rejected Jehovah, and they have reared their own gods. The first five years of Jeremiah's ministry were before the Book of the Law was found. During this time King Josiah, who was a young man like Jeremiah, was seeking the Lord and instituting certain reforms in the nation. Primarily, he was trying to clean up the idolatry in Judah. The nation had forsaken the living God and had gone over into idolatry.

It would be difficult to find any portion of Scripture that would surpass Jeremiah's message in genuine pa-

thos and tenderness. It is the eloquent and earnest plead-
ing of a God who has been forgotten and insulted. His
grace and compassion toward the guilty nation are
blended with solemn warnings of dreadful days to come
if hearts were not turned back to Him:

> **Moreover the word of the LORD came to me, saying,
> Go and cry in the hearing of Jerusalem, saying, Thus
> saith the LORD, I remember thee. . . .** (Jeremiah 2:1,
> 2)

"I remember thee . . . ," God says. The people had forgotten Him, but God had not forgotten them. Oh, how gracious God is! Listen to His longing:

> **Israel was holiness unto the LORD, and the first
> fruits of his increase; all that devour him shall of-
> fend; evil shall come upon them, saith the LORD.** (Jer-
> emiah 2:3)

In other words, "Israel, once you were holiness unto the
Lord. Don't you remember back then how you were? You
belonged to Me. You followed Me, and I led you and protected you from your enemies." Jeremiah continues:

> **Hear ye the word of the LORD, O house of Jacob, and
> all the families of the house of Israel. Thus saith the
> LORD, What iniquity have your fathers found in me,
> that they are gone far from me, and have walked
> after vanity, and are become vain?** (Jeremiah 2:4, 5)

Notice the wonderful way in which God approached
them: "What did I do wrong that you have turned from
Me?" In our day, my friend, what is wrong with God that
we are not more interested in Him? Why are we not

serving Him? Is there unrighteousness with God? Is God doing something wrong today? He asks, "What iniquity have your fathers found in Me?"

> **Neither said they, Where is the LORD who brought us up out of the land of Egypt, who led us through the wilderness, through a land of deserts and of pits, through a land of drought, and of the shadow of death, through a land that no man passed through, and where no man dwelt? And I brought you into a plentiful country, to eat its fruit and its goodness, but when ye entered, ye defiled my land, and made mine heritage an abomination.** (Jeremiah 2:6, 7)

People just avoided that country, and there are not many who go through it today. I have been at the edge of it, and that is as far as I wanted to go. Yet God kept His people in that frightful wilderness for forty years, and He took care of them.

Now He says, "What did you do? You defiled My land!" We hear a great deal about ecology and the fact that we need to clean up the land. That is good—it needs cleaning up. But let's recognize that there is a lot of moral filth around, and a lot of degradation and deterioration in character. This is the thing that the Lord God is talking about here. They had polluted God's land. God intended that the Israelites be a witness to Him; instead they were as bad as the people before them.

> **The priests said not, Where is the LORD? And they that handle the law knew me not. The rulers also transgressed against me, and the prophets prophesied by Baal, and walked after things that do not profit.** (Jeremiah 2:8)

God puts the responsibility on the spiritual leaders. And I believe that the problems in our own country began in the church. No nation falls until it falls first spiritually. There is first of all a spiritual apostasy, then a moral awfulness, and finally a political anarchy. That is the way every great nation makes its exit from greatness.

"The priests said not, Where is the LORD?" There are too many folk today who are supposed to be Bible teachers and preachers and witnesses for Him, even among the laity, who do not know the Word of God. I am sorry to say that, but it happens to be true. As a result of not knowing the Word of God, they don't really know God. It is necessary to know the Word of God in order to know Him.

I know of no book that fits into the present hour with a message that is better for us than this Book of Jeremiah. After World War II there was a little wave of revival. There were several evangelists out at that time, and the crowds came. During that time I began my weekly Bible studies which drew a large audience from miles around. And at that time we would hear pastors say that church attendance had doubled and tripled. They were putting chairs in the aisles and building new buildings. They mistook growth in numbers for spiritual growth and development. This is the point that Jeremiah was making.

People today still think there is something valuable in great religious splurges and conventions. This type of thing doesn't appeal to me, because I am not an organization man, nor am I a joiner. But some people love organizations and conventions. The problem is that some people mistake enthusiasm for a moving of the Spirit of God. Now I will probably be as unpopular as Jeremiah when I say that is not revival. Nothing is true revival unless it transforms lives.

The Wesleyan movement in England changed lives. It just about put the liquor industry out of business in England. It changed conditions in factories and resulted in the enactment of child labor laws. It was a spiritual movement that reached into the lives of the people. I want to see a spiritual movement today that will reach into the ghetto. When the government reaches into the ghetto with so-called social reform as we have it today, there is crookedness and misappropriation of funds, and nothing is made right. What we need is true revival, which is the only thing that will really change the ghetto.

That was the message of Jeremiah in his day. You can see how unpopular that young man must have been as he stood there delivering God's message. I can picture him there—a lonely fellow, heartbroken at the message of doom he was giving to his people when they refused to repent. But he was giving it faithfully, and it did bring partial revival.

As Jeremiah gives his message in the gate of the Lord's house, he shows them how foolish idolatry is.

Hear the word which the Lord speaketh unto you, O house of Israel. Thus saith the Lord, Learn not the way of the nations, and be not dismayed at the signs of heaven; for the nations are dismayed at them. For the customs of the people are vain: for one cutteth a tree out of the forest, the work of the hands of the workman, with the axe. They deck it with silver and with gold; they fasten it with nails and with hammers, that it move not. They [these man-made idols] **are upright like the palm tree, but speak not; they must needs be borne, because they cannot go. Be not afraid of them; for they cannot do evil, neither also is it in them to do good. Forasmuch as there is none like unto thee, O Lord; thou art**

great, and thy name is great in might. (Jeremiah 10:1–6)

Here we see that the people were substituting something for God.

People have always had substitutes for God. Anyone who is not worshiping the true and living God has some substitute for Him. It may be that the person himself becomes his god—there are a great number of people who actually worship themselves. Others worship money and are willing to be dishonest to become rich. Others worship fame and will sell their honor in order to obtain some unworthy goal. There are many substitutes for God, and Jeremiah talks about this here.

Notice what he says, ". . . be not dismayed at the signs of heaven. . . ." People today are still doing what they did in the time of Jeremiah, trying to regulate their lives by the zodiac. They want to know what sign they were born under and all that nonsense. It is given out through our news media as though it were genuine! My friend, the astrology that is being promoted today is something which has been picked up from the pagan world.

"The customs of the peoples are vain"—they are empty. Jeremiah is ridiculing with bitter irony the idolatry of his day—going out to the woods, cutting down a tree, shaping it into an image, decorating it with silver and gold—and that's their god! It is like worshiping a scarecrow!

Jeremiah turns the eyes of the people toward the Lord Himself: "There is none like unto thee, O Lord; thou art great, and thy name is great in might." The Lord cannot be compared to anything. How ridiculous it is to turn from the true and living God to worship the things around you and get your leading from the demonic world!

Thus shall ye say unto them, The gods that have not made the heavens and the earth, even they shall perish from the earth, and from under these heavens. (Jeremiah 10:11)

The gods of the heathen did not create the universe. Our God, the living God, created it.

He hath made the earth by his power; he hath established the world by his wisdom, and hath stretched out the heavens by his understanding. (Jeremiah 10:12)

The stars are up there in their places because God put them there. He placed them where He wanted them. He didn't ask you or me how we wanted them arranged. This is His universe, and He is the only One who is worthy of our worship. We may smile at the people of previous centuries who cut down a tree to make a god. We call ourselves intelligent and civilized; yet our people spend millions of dollars to try to discern their future from occult sources who may claim to speak for God—channelers, psychics, gurus, spirit guides, ouija boards, shamans, mediums, etc. If people today are so intelligent, why don't they worship the living and true God and get into reality?

No man can walk aright apart from the revelation of God in His Word:

O Lord, I know that the way of man is not in himself; it is not in man that walketh to direct his steps. (Jeremiah 10:23)

The minute a man turns from the Word of God, he is on a detour. That is our natural course. In fact, we begin that way as children. I used to take my little grandson for a stroll around the block when he was learning to walk. He was a wonderful little fellow, but he wore me out because he wanted to walk up the sidewalk of every house we passed, or to run out in the street. And when we would get to a corner he would want to go the wrong way. I have never seen a little fellow who wanted to go in as many wrong ways as he did. One day when we finally got home, I said to him, "Kim, you're just like your grandfather. When he gets away from the Word of God he always goes down a detour." My friend, it is not in man to direct his own steps. We are dependent upon the omniscient God for direction in every area of our lives.

The Downward Path

From the beginning, man knew there was only one God. How did it happen that idolatry has taken over the great masses of humanity in the world? Paul answers that question in Romans 1:21-23 where we see that there are seven steps which mankind took downward from the Garden of Eden:

Because, when they knew God, they glorified him not as God, neither were thankful, but became vain in their imaginations, and their foolish heart was darkened. Professing themselves to be wise, they became fools, and changed the glory of the incorruptible God into an image made like corruptible man, and birds, and four-footed beasts, and creeping things.

There is no such thing as man moving upward. These verses contradict the hypothesis of evolution. Man is not improving physically, morally, intellectually, or spiritually. The pull is downward. Of course, this contradicts all the anthologies of religion that start with man in a very primitive condition as a caveman with very little intellectual qualities and move him up intellectually and begin moving him toward God. This is absolute error. Man is moving away from God, and right now the world is probably farther from God than at any time in its history.

The fact of the matter is that every primitive tribe has a tradition that way back in the beginning their ancestors knew God. But no people have ever lived up to the light that they have had. Although they had a knowledge of God, they moved away from Him. "They glorified him not as God." They did not give Him His rightful place, and man became self-sufficient. In our day man has made the announcement that God is dead. In the beginning the human family did not suggest that God was dead, they simply turned their backs upon Him and made man their god.

They "became vain in their imaginations"—they even concocted a theory of evolution.

"Their foolish heart was darkened"; that is, they moved into the darkness of paganism. You see living proof of this as you walk down the streets of Cairo in Egypt or of Istanbul in Turkey. In fact, all you have to do is walk down the streets of Los Angeles or New York— or of your own hometown—to know that man's foolish heart is darkened.

"Professing themselves to be wise, they became fools." The wisdom of man is foolishness with God. Man searches for truth through logical reasoning but arrives at a philosophy that is foolish in God's sight.

"And changed the glory of the incorruptible God into an image made like corruptible man, and birds, and four-footed beasts, and creeping things." Have you noted that the unsaved world has made caricatures of God? Look at the images and the idols of the heathen. I was aware of this during my visit to the ruins of the ancient city of Ephesus. That city in the Roman Empire reached probably the highest degree of culture in civilization that any city has ever reached. Yet at the heart of that city was one of the most horrible images imaginable, enshrined in the temple of Artemis, one of the seven wonders of the ancient world. Also called Diana, she was not the lovely image you see in Greek sculptures. She was like the oriental Cybele, the mother goddess, the many-breasted one. She had a trident in one hand and in the other a club—she was a mean one! That is the idea the most cultured, civilized people had of God! She was a female principal, and gross immorality took place around her temple and dishonesty of the worst sort. They had turned the glory of the incorruptible God into the likeness of an image of corruptible mankind.

Actually, idolatry is a cartoon of God; it is a slander and a slur against Him. Personally I do not like to see pictures of Jesus, as Paul said that we know Him no longer "after the flesh" (see 2 Corinthians 5:16). He is the glorified Christ. He is not that picture you have hanging on your wall, my friend. If He came into your room, you would fall on your face before Him. He is the glorified Christ today. Don't slur our God by having a picture of Him! The Greeks made their gods like themselves with their own imperfections; the Assyrians and the Egyptians and the Babylonians made their gods like beasts and birds and creeping things. I walked through the museum in Cairo and looked at some of the gods they had made. They are not very flattering representations, I can assure you.

Man did not begin in idolatry. The savage of today is very unlike primitive man. Primitive man was monotheistic; idolatry was introduced later. In the Word of God the first record we have of idolatry is in connection with Rachel stealing her father's idols (Genesis 31). Man descended downward; he did not develop upward. Religiously, man has departed from God. Sir William Ramsay, who was once a belligerent unbeliever, wrote in his book *The Cities of Paul,*

> For my own part, I confess that my experience and reading show nothing to confirm the modern assumptions in religious history, and a great deal to confirm Paul. Whatever evidence exists, with the rarest exceptions, the history of religion among men is a history of degeneration. . . . The fact of human history [is] that man, standing alone, degenerates; and that he progresses only where there is in him so much sympathy with and devotion to the Divine life as to keep the social body pure and sweet and healthy.

My friend, the reason today there is failure in our poverty programs and health programs and other social programs is because of gross immorality and a turning away from God. They say, "We want to be practical, and we do not want to introduce religion." That's the problem. The only practical thing for man to do is to return to the living and true God.

In spite of the fact that the people of Israel made a covenant to serve God during the reign of King Josiah, the revival in the land proved to be largely a surface movement. There is no question that the words of Jeremiah had their effect and that there were some who gen-

uinely turned to the Lord. However, things in the nation
were deteriorating. After the revival, interest in spiritual
things began to wear off again and the people returned
to their old ways. That which followed was a very evil
period in the life of the nation. Josiah had been slain,
Jeremiah had been forced to leave his hometown, and
evil men had come to the throne.

**The sin of Judah is written with a pen of iron, and
with the point of a diamond; it is engraved upon the
tablet of their heart, and upon the horns of your
altars, while their children remember their altars
and their idols by the green trees upon the high hills.**
(Jeremiah 17:1, 2)

There was evil in everything the people of Judah did. It
even permeated their religion.

How It Ends

Dr. W. G. Moorehead has given us this very graphic
picture of Jeremiah:

It was Jeremiah's lot to prophesy at a time when all
things in Judah were rushing down to the final and
mournful catastrophe; when political excitement was
at its height; when the worst passions swayed the various parties, and the most fatal counsels prevailed. It
was his to stand in the way over which his nation was
rushing headlong to destruction; to make an heroic
effort to arrest it, and to turn it back; and to fail, and
be compelled to step to one side and see his own people, whom he loved with the tenderness of a woman,
plunge over the precipice into the wide, weltering ruin.

Jeremiah lived to see the destruction of Jerusalem and the Babylonian captivity. He mourned the destruction of Jerusalem, standing alone amid the ashes weeping.

Is it nothing to you, all ye that pass by? Behold, and see if there be any sorrow like unto my sorrow. . . . Hear, I pray you, all people, and behold my sorrow; my virgins and my young men are gone into captivity. (Lamentations 1:12,18)

The people of Israel had listened to the wrong voices, and we have done the same thing in our own recent history. Gladstone, the great English jurist, was asked what was the mark of a great statesman. He gave this answer: "A great statesman is a man who knows the direction God is moving for the next fifty years." My friend, we certainly have not had leaders like that. As a result we have missed a great opportunity as a nation for leadership in the world, and the great middle class of our nation has been corrupted. We are headed down just as Israel went down. We have refused to listen to the Word of God.

Why had Jerusalem been destroyed? The city had sinned. The second explanation is, the Lord is righteous. God did it, and God was right in what He did. This is difficult to understand, and I must say I feel totally inadequate to deal with it. Obviously Jeremiah is entering into the sorrow of our Lord Himself for the people He is chastening, much like He did six centuries later when He wept over Jerusalem:

O Jerusalem, Jerusalem, thou that killest the prophets, and stonest them who are sent unto thee, how often would I have gathered thy children together,

even as a hen gathereth her chickens under her wings, and ye would not! (Matthew 23:37)

I merely stand at the fringe of this sorrow and find I cannot enter in.

A statement from G. Campbell Morgan may help us to understand the revelation of God's anger:

> This is a supreme necessity in the interest of the universe. Prisons are in the interest of the free. Hell is the safeguard of heaven. A State that cannot punish crime is doomed; and a God Who tolerates evil is not good. Deny me my Biblical revelation of the anger of God, and I am insecure in the universe. But reveal to me this Throne established, occupied by One Whose heart is full of tenderness, whose bowels yearn with love; then I am assured that He will not tolerate that which blights and blasts and damns; but will destroy it, and all its instruments, in the interest of that which is high and noble and pure. (*Studies in the Prophecy of Jeremiah*, p. 248)

You and I are living in a universe where there is the almighty, eternal God, the living God whose heart goes out in love and yearning over you. But I want to say this to you: If you turn your back on Him, He will judge you even though He still loves you. He is the righteous God of this universe. I am not sure I understand all this, but as Dr. Morgan has put it, I know it is what He says in His Word. Someday He will make it clear to us that hell is actually there because He is a God of love and a God of righteousness and a God of holiness. At that time the whole universe, including Satan himself, will admit that God is righteous and just in all He does.

In these first two of the Ten Commandments which deal with man's relationship with Himself, God says:

Thou shalt have no other gods before me. Thou shalt not make unto thee any carved image, or any likeness of anything that is in heaven above, or that is in the earth beneath, or that is in the water under the earth; thou shalt not bow down thyself to them, nor serve them; for I, the Lord thy God am a jealous God, visiting the iniquity of the fathers upon the children unto the third and fourth generation of them that hate me; and showing mercy unto thousands of them that love me, and keep my commandments. (Exodus 20:3–6)

My friend, God is so great and wonderful and good we dare not trifle with Him.

CHAPTER 3

THE NAME OF THE LORD
The Third Commandment

Thou shalt not take the name of the LORD thy God in vain; for the LORD will not hold him guiltless that taketh his name in vain. (Exodus 20:7)

You and I are living in a day when the human family assumes they can take God's name in vain and get by with it. But that's not what God's Word tells us! Notice Exodus 20:7 again. The first statement is the commandment. Then the second statement adds a warning. This warning is not a threat nor is it menacing in any sense—but it is the statement of an axiom of truth, an eternal fact. It reveals an awful sanction, and it is a solemn assertion which adds to the importance of the commandment: God will not hold a man guiltless who takes His name in vain.

When we turn to Leviticus 24:10-14 we will discover the penalty that was imposed upon those who did take God's name in vain:

And the son of an Israelitish woman, whose father was an Egyptian, went out among the children of Israel. And this son of the Israelitish woman and a man of Israel strove together in the camp; and the Israelitish woman's son blasphemed the name of the LORD, and cursed. And they brought him unto Moses (and his mother's name was Shelomith, the daughter of Dibri, of the tribe of Dan), and they put him in

prison, that the mind of the LORD might be shown them. And the LORD spoke unto Moses, saying, Bring forth him who hath cursed outside the camp; and let all that heard him lay their hands upon his head, and let all the congregation stone him.

Now turn over to the Book of Deuteronomy and note God's care in determining actual guilt:

One witness shall not rise up against a man for any iniquity, or for any sin, in any sin that he sinneth; at the mouth of two witnesses, or at the mouth of three witnesses, shall the matter be established. If a false witness rise up against any man to testify against him that which is wrong, then both the men, between whom the controversy is, shall stand before the LORD, before the priests and the judges, who shall be in those days; and the judges shall make diligent inquiry; and, behold, if the witness be a false witness, and hath testified falsely against his brother, then shall ye do unto him, as he had thought to have done unto his brother. So shalt thou put the evil away from among you. (Deuteronomy 19:15–19)

For men who would perjure themselves, the death penalty was inflicted. Nothing that could be meted out was more severe.

As we emphasize the importance of this third commandment, first of all, let's see what the commandment means. Perhaps a slight difference in the translation might clarify it: "Thou shalt not bring the name of Jehovah, thy Elohim, to a vanity or to emptiness by your life or your speech. Do not reduce God's name down to where it is meaningless to those who are around you in your walk in life."

Now the names of God tell us something about God. Whole volumes have been written on this subject alone, but let me just say that the names of God tell us something about the reality of God—things which in our own finiteness we know as real. They tell us something about the character of God, about His wonderful attributes: that our God is holy, our God is righteous, our God is love, our God is merciful. Our God is omnipotent—He has absolute power. He is omnipresent—present in all places at all times. And He is omniscient—that is, He has perfect knowledge. Also our God is immutable, unchangeable. These names tell us something about the wonder, the glory and the reality of our God. Scripture attaches great significance to the name of God.

If you will go back to the very beginning of the human family and break into the story just after Cain had killed his brother Abel and was driven from the presence of the Lord, you will find at that God raised up another son, Seth. We read that when God raised up Seth and he became a father, "then began men to call upon the name of the LORD" (Genesis 4:26). And then God's name meant a great deal.

Have you ever realized the importance of the name of God to the nation Israel? In Leviticus 24:16 our translation reads:

And he who blasphemeth the name of the LORD [Jehovah], he shall surely be put to death . . .

Actually, the Septuagint, which is the Greek translation of the Old Testament made by the seventy (or 72) elders from Jerusalem in about the second century B.C., translates this passage as follows: "He that nameth the name of the LORD shall surely be put to death." This is the reason that scholars disagree as to the pronunciation of Jehovah (the name translated LORD in the King James Version). Some want to call His name Yahweh while other scholars want to use different translations. You ask, "Why can't they agree on the pronunciation of this word?" The reason is that Israel did not pronounce the name of the Lord—His name was so holy to these people that they did not speak it. What a commentary on the present generation when His name is carelessly mouthed in practically every sentence, and sometimes even by Christians!

A tremendous importance is given to the name of God in the Scriptures. For example, you will find this expressed in Psalm 91:14:

Because he hath set his love upon me, therefore will I deliver him; I will set him on high, because he hath known my name.

Then, in Malachi, the last book of the Old Testament, we read:

Then they that feared the LORD spoke often one to another: and the LORD hearkened, and heard it, and a book of remembrance was written before him for them that feared the LORD, and that thought upon his name. (Malachi 3:16)

And in Psalm 9:10 you will find:

And they who know thy name will put their trust in thee; for thou, LORD [Jehovah], hast not forsaken those who seek thee.

May I say to you that the name of God became wonderfully holy and significant to these people!

Let us look at just one other Scripture which reveals that there was a time when Israel became careless with His name:

Hear ye this, O house of Jacob, who are called by the name of Israel, and are come forth out of the waters of Judah; who swear by the name of the LORD [Jehovah], and make mention of the God of Israel, but not in truth, nor in righteousness. (Isaiah 48:1)

And that, my friend, was to profane the name of God, and Isaiah called it to their attention "You mention His name, but not in truth, nor in righteousness." That was to blaspheme!

The New Testament sums up the adoration and worship in which we are to hold His name. We see this in the prayer our Lord taught His disciples to pray, saying:

Our Father, who art in heaven, Hallowed be thy name. (Matthew 6:9)

Scripture does not treat lightly the name of God.

We need to consider three ways in which you and I are most likely to take God's name in vain.

We can take God's name in vain by profanity.
We can take God's name in vain by perjury.
We can take God's name in vain by perfidy.

The Sin of Profanity

Now we want to examine all three of these carefully. And we shall deal with the first one with gloves off, because this is the prevailing sin and popular vice of

America today—the vice of profanity. It is a creeping paralysis in the very heart of a nation and a society. It will eventually destroy the moral fiber of a nation and will corrupt the language of any people who take God's name in vain.

George Washington took a stand on this, and we would do well to read again a notation of this great man as entered in his orderly book of August 3, 1776:

> The General is sorry to be informed that the foolish and wicked practice of profane swearing, a vice hitherto little known in the American army, is growing into fashion. . . . He hopes the officers will, by example as well as influence, endeavor to check it, and that both they and the men will reflect that we can have little hope of the blessing of heaven on our arms if we insult it by our impiety and profanity. Added to this, it's a vice so mean and low, without temptation, that every man of sense and character detests and despises it.

That's a rare statement in this day, is it not? After World War I the floodgates of profanity were opened in America. Then, after World War II, it was given another and greater impetus until today it has become a popular vice that is more or less accepted in the world.

Some men and women are so impoverished in their vocabularies that they seem to feel the need to color their language with profanity. Others are so disgustingly unimpressive that they feel the need of a salty conversation with mouth-swelling oaths. I am not implying that all who use profanity are morons, although a good number are. We observe that there are intelligent men and women who are addicted to this habit today, but we can certainly add this: when they use profanity they are not involving the use of their intelligence.

We are living in a day when the majority of Americans think they can take God's name in vain and get by with it. I picked up the following summary some time ago:

Science seems to have made God unnecessary.
Philosophy seems to have made God impossible.
Psychology seems to have made God an illusion.
Communism has attempted to make Him an enemy of mankind.
Capitalism has used Him as merely a convenience.
And realistic novelists and playwrights use Him only to enlarge their vocabulary of profanity.

However, it needs to be said, and I shall say it today, that historically swearing is the language of morons, criminals, gangsters and prostitutes. They are the ones who use it—it is their language, and a man or woman who dishonors God's name is adopting their language, my beloved.

In Shakespeare's *The Tempest*, we read that when Prospero was able to capture the savage Caliban, he taught him how to speak, and this is the comment of Caliban: "You taught me language; and my profit on't is, I know how to curse." And cursing is about all some folk in our day seem to know.

Robert Hall, one of the great preachers of yesteryear, said this concerning profanity:

It's difficult to account for a practice which gratifies no passion, and promotes no interest, unless we ascribe it to a certain vanity of appearing superior to religious fear.

Profanity is a symbol of spiritual sickness. It's a symbol of moral bankruptcy and breakdown. It reveals that there is a poisoned fountain somewhere. I can illustrate this in a very homely and ugly incident of a dirty epithet that reflects upon a man's mother, an insult that no man will take. In the east some time ago, a young man was talking to me at a filling station, and he applied this contemptuous epithet to himself several times during the conversation. Now, the fact that he said that of himself is no proof that his mother was a cheap and vulgar woman, but it is proof that he was a cheap and vulgar man to talk that way about his mother.

Also, I remember when I was a boy—I don't think I was over six years of age—I used to hang around the cotton gin operated by my dad. I do not believe men ever get more foulmouthed than those men did. And to this good day I can remember one man who got married, and when he came back to work, the fellows started kidding him. I'll never forget till my dying day the vulgar, crude things he said about his wife. And even as a six-year-old boy I despised him, and to this day I despise him. A man who will talk about his mother or his wife like he did is low. And, my friend, if it is low to speak about your mother, your sister or your wife like that, it's ten thousand times worse to speak about God like that!

Somebody says, "Well, I do it, but I don't mean anything by it." Do you mean to tell me that you think nothing of trifling with the name of your Creator? Do you mean to tell me you're using language so loosely, when God has said He will not hold you guiltless? Do you believe Him, or don't you believe Him? God says He will not hold you guiltless if you take His name in vain.

Now there is another common expression that people use today—they ask God to damn some person or thing. Some can hardly speak without the use of this phrase. And just here let me call attention to the fact that in uttering this request that God damn someone, you are uttering a prayer, and it is an awful prayer to ask God to damn a person. Also, when asking God to do this, you misrepresent God. What an awful libel it is upon our holy God! My friend, God is not in the damning business. He is in the saving business! God is saving, not damning folk, and if you are lost, you are lost because you choose to be lost. If you walk out of a house of worship or tune out a gospel message on the radio, it is because you willfully turn your back on God. God's will is that none should perish but that all might come to the knowledge of the truth.

Let's listen to the apostle Peter as he speaks of this:

Neither is there salvation in any other; for there is no other name under heaven given among men, whereby we must be saved. (Acts 4:12)

God's name is not a name to damn anyone, it is the only name that can save you. Profanity is condemned of God and, my friend, He hasn't changed His mind in our permissive age. He says He will not hold you guiltless.

The Sin of Perjury

Then there's another way in which God's name is taken in vain. It is by perjury. We find a case of perjury in an experience of Elisha, who in my judgment was one of the greatest prophets of all. We read in 2 Kings 8, beginning with verse 7, that when Elisha went to Damascus, the capital of Syria, he received an urgent message from the king:

And Elisha came to Damascus; and Ben-hadad, the king of Syria, was sick, and it was told him, saying,

The man of God is come here. And the king said unto Hazael, Take a present in thine hand, and go, meet the man of God, and inquire of the LORD by him, saying, Shall I recover from this disease? So Hazael went to meet him, and took a present with him . . . and came and stood before him, and said, Thy son, Ben-hadad, king of Syria, hath sent me to thee, saying, Shall I recover from this disease? And Elisha said unto him, Go, say unto him, Thou mayest certainly recover. Howbeit, the LORD hath showed me that he shall surely die. (vv.7-10)

"You will surely live, but you won't live." That sounds like double-talk. But Hazael already knew that he would be the king's successor to the throne, and the king's death was what he wanted.

And he settled his countenance steadfastly, until he was ashamed; and the man of God wept. And Hazael said, Why weepeth my lord? (vv. 11,12)

Elisha's knowing eyes bored into him until Hazael felt embarrassed. Then Elisha began to weep. God revealed to Elisha that Hazael would not only murder the king, but when he came to the throne he would be a brutal enemy of Israel.

And he answered, Because I know the evil that thou wilt do unto the children of Israel: their strongholds wilt thou set on fire, and their young men wilt thou slay with the sword, and wilt dash their children, and rip up their women with child. And Hazael said, But what is thy servant, a dog, that he should do this great thing? (vv. 12,13)

I don't know if he was a dog or not, but he did perjure himself in the presence of God's prophet.

> **And Elisha answered, The LORD hath shown me that thou shalt be king over Syria. So he departed from Elisha, and came to his master, who said to him, What said Elisha to thee? And he answered, He told me that thou shouldest surely recover. And it came to pass on the next day, that he took a thick cloth, and dipped it in water, and spread it on his face, so that he died; and Hazael reigned in his stead.** (vv. 13–15)

There in the very presence of this man who was God's mouthpiece he perjured himself and said in essence, "I will not do this," when at that very moment he planned to do it. That is to take God's name in vain.

To ask God to be witness to a lie seems to be almost an unpardonable sin, if there is an unpardonable sin. Even among the heathen down through the centuries they have always held that a man should never go against his oath.

Philo, one of the greatest of Greek writers, left us this: "To invoke God to attest the truth of a lie is a most impious deed." And then he went on, speaking very personally, "You ask God to bear witness to the truth of my lie, aid me in my wrongdoing and help me in my crime."

We may not use profanity, but it is possible that we have agreed to do some service for the Lord, have taken it lightly and not done it. If so, we have taken God's name in vain. Perhaps we have taken an office and we are not performing the duties of that office faithfully. If we are not serious in the acceptance of that position, then we have taken God's name in vain. Have we promised that we would do something and not carried it out? That is to take His name in vain. When we do something after this manner, it is nothing in the world but practical atheism—it is to act as if God were not around when we said it. My friend, whoever you are, wherever you are, remember: "The eyes of the LORD are in every place, beholding the evil and the good" (Proverbs 15:3). Solomon wrote that proverb, for he found that our God is an all-seeing God.

The psalmist wrote,

> **The LORD looketh from heaven; he beholdeth all the sons of men. From the place of his habitation he looketh upon all the inhabitants of the earth.** (Psalm 33:13,14)

And the writer of the Book of Hebrews put it like this:

> **Neither is there any creature that is not manifest in his sight, but all things are naked and opened unto the eyes of him with whom we have to do.** (Hebrews 4:13)

And finally,

> **For God shall bring every work into judgment, with every secret thing, whether it be good, or whether it be evil.** (Ecclesiastes 12:14)

We must keep reminding ourselves, "The LORD will not hold him guiltless that taketh his name in vain." Also, remember that it is nothing short of practical atheism to take an oath or to promise something in the Lord's work and then not make good.

Then, friend, to live a lie is perjury. The very name Christian designates our acceptance of Christ—therefore, living a lie is to take God's name in vain. Plainly, it is to say or do or pretend something that we really are not.

There is the story of a donkey who suddenly became rich and felt he was too good to associate with the other donkeys. So he went to the beauty shop and had his ears trimmed and then pinned down. With this improvement he began going with the horses. He was a little uncomfortable at first, but he did not want to associate with donkeys anymore. And then one day the horses called on him to sing. The minute he did, he gave himself away and was driven out from association with the horses because, you see, he was pretending to be something he was not.

From the barnyard also comes this little poem from an unknown author:

> *A jolly old sow once lived in a sty,*
> *And three little piggies had she.*
> *She waddled about saying, "Oink, oink, oink,"*
> *While the little ones said, "Wee, wee."*
> *"My dear little brothers," said one of the brats,*
> *"My dear little piggies," said he,*
> *"Let us all, for the future, say, 'Oink, oink, oink,'*
> *It's so childish to say, 'Wee, wee.'"*
>
> *These three little piggies grew skinny and lean,*
> *And lean they might very well be,*
> *For somehow they couldn't say, "Oink, oink, oink,"*
> *And they wouldn't say, "Wee, wee, wee."*
>
> *And after awhile these little pigs died,*
> *They all died of felo-de-se,*
> *From trying so hard to say, "Oink, oink, oink,"*
> *When they only could say, "Wee, wee."*

Oh, friend, for you and me today it is perjury to sing or

to say something or appear to be something that we are not. That is to take God's name in vain.

The Sin of Perfidy

The last sin that we'll mention is taking God's name in vain by perfidy. By perfidy is meant an act of violating faith. It has a flippant and frivolous note to it, and it means a flippant and frivolous attitude toward God and sacred things.

The Lord Jesus Christ gave this parable of two sons:

A certain man had two sons; and he came to the first, and said, Son, go work today in my vineyard. He answered and said, I will not; but afterward he repented, and went. And he came to the second, and said the same. And he answered and said, I go, sir; and went not. Which of the two did the will of his father? They say unto him, The first. Jesus saith unto them, Verily I say unto you that the tax collectors and the harlots go into the kingdom of God before you. (Matthew 21:28–31)

Now let's look at what our Lord is telling us here. The father came and said to one son, "I want you to go work today in my vineyard." And the boy said, "I will not go." Oh, the insolent indifference of that boy to the father! He's guilty of perjury. But later on he repented and went. Then the second son, when he received the command, smoothly and soothingly said, "I go," but he did not. He perjured himself also, but more than that, he was guilty of perfidy—he was substituting a profession for practice. He treated as commonplace the things that were sacred.

My beloved, are we guilty of trampling in the dirt the

holy will of our Father? To do so is perfidy, and that is what it means to take the name of God in vain. This is what Dr. G. Campbell Morgan meant when he wrote, "I am more afraid of the blasphemy of the sanctuary than the blasphemy of the street."

And this is perfidy, to treat holy things as if they were commonplace. It's to leave, as it were, the shoes on our feet when we are on holy ground—holy in the sense of being set apart for the worship of God. It's to be frivolous when we should not be frivolous. Sometimes the familiarity with the church and with God's Word may breed contempt in our hearts and carelessness in our lives toward things which are very serious to God.

My friend, this is a danger church members face. And this is a danger to this poor preacher today. I repeatedly remind myself of this when I walk into a pulpit. I dare not stand there without being faithful to the trust given to me and reminding myself, *This is a holy spot!* And we in a congregation dare not sit there in church and treat as frivolous the things of God. To sit there slovenly, idly, unattentive and dozing is to take God's name in vain. We need to teach our children today that there's something shocking about levity, vanity and irreverence in God's presence.

Oh, the blasphemy of singing praises in a meaningless fashion or making bold promises before God that we do not intend to keep and going out to contradict them by our lives! Prayer without practice is blasphemy, and praise without worship is taking God's name in vain.

It would be well to ask ourselves: Why do I go to church? Do I go from force of habit? Do I go for show or for pretence or for performance? Or do I really go to worship God? Our Lord says,

Many will say to me in that day, Lord, Lord, have we not prophesied in thy name? And in thy name have

cast out demons? And in thy name done many wonderful works? And then will I profess unto them, I never knew you. . . . (Matthew 7:22, 23)

To trifle with God is serious. God says, "I'll not hold you guiltless if you take My name in vain." When we do so, even here and now, our spiritual life ebbs out. We are bleeding spiritually. Our conscience becomes seared as with a hot iron. We can come into God's presence and walk out of God's presence without being affected, and our lives are never transformed. That, my friend, is worse than swearing on the streets. And to assume the name of Christian without trusting Jesus as Savior—that is to take His name in vain. Remember that when God brought Jesus into the world, the instructions were, "Thou shalt call his name JESUS; for he shall save his people from their sins" (Matthew 1:21).

You say, "Preacher, that's a strong message." Yes, it is, but somebody needs to declare it today, because a great many people are blaspheming God's name, and a great many are taking His name in vain without realizing it. My friend, do you dare stand and look into the face of heaven and honestly say, "God, I have never blasphemed Your name, and I have never taken Your name in vain"? If you can do that, then you can get into heaven by keeping this commandment—provided you keep the other nine also. If you look down into your heart today, I believe you will be forced to admit that you have taken His name in vain.

Well, what are you going to do? Are you going to be saved by keeping the Ten Commandments? My beloved, remember that poor publican who stood off at a distance and beat upon his breast and said, "God, be merciful to me, a sinner!" Actually, he didn't really say it quite that way. He said, "Oh, God, for me a publican, if there were only a mercy seat!" You see, because he had turned his back on God, he had been shut out from the mercy seat in the temple. He couldn't get in.

Oh, I'm glad to tell you that God has already made a mercy seat for every sinner—for you and for me and for everyone! What we want and what we need today is mercy. And God is prepared to extend mercy if we are honest with Him, if we are willing to come and say, "Lord, I've fallen short of Thy glory. I cast myself upon Thy mercy." Then we will hear Him say,

Come now, and let us reason together, saith the LORD: though your sins be as scarlet, they shall be as white as snow; though they be red like crimson, they shall be as wool. (Isaiah 1:18)

You see, God says that the blood of Jesus Christ, His Son, cleanses us from all sin—even the sin of taking His name in vain.

CHAPTER 4

THE SABBATH DAY OR THE LORD'S DAY—WHICH?
The Fourth Commandment

Remember the sabbath day, to keep it holy. Six days shalt thou labor and do all thy work; but the seventh day is the sabbath of the LORD thy God; in it thou shalt not do any work, thou, nor thy son, nor thy daughter, thy manservant, nor thy maidservant, nor thy cattle, nor thy stranger that is within thy gates; for in six days the LORD made heaven and earth, the sea, and all that in them is, and rested the seventh day; wherefore, the LORD blessed the sabbath day, and hallowed it. (Exodus 20:8–11)

The Sabbath day is Saturday. It is the seventh day of the week according to our calendar. Furthermore, the Sabbath day has never been changed to Sunday.

The present-day controversy hinges upon a false premise which resulted in a warped and distorted viewpoint of the real meaning of the Sabbath day as found in the Word of God. Many Christians have a woeful misconception of why the church has always observed the first day of the week. Nothing but abysmal ignorance has permitted the protagonists of the Sabbath day to traffic in their legalistic system.

Now this question today, "When was the Sabbath changed to Sunday?" is like the old chestnut asked by the man who was very much a Mr. Milquetoast: "Do you still beat your wife?" You cannot answer that question without getting into a peck of trouble. If you say, "Yes," you are wrong. If you say, "No," you are wrong, and you are immediately in difficulty. For the same reason, "When was the Sabbath day changed to Sunday?" is one of those questions that cannot be answered with a yes or no since it is based upon a false premise.

I am going to ask that you think with me as I deal with this subject, for I believe this to be one of the most important of the commandments, and it is essential that we understand what it means.

The Ten Commandments are given first in Exodus 20. They are repeated in Deuteronomy 5, but it is interesting to note that in no instance is this a repetition of the Law—it is rather an interpretation of the Law in the lives of the people and nation after forty years of experience with it in the wilderness. Therefore, all the commandments that we find given in Deuteronomy are identical with those given in Exodus with one exception, the fourth commandment, the one that has to do with the Sabbath day. Thereby hangs a tale, and this is something our legalistic friends never call to our attention.

Basis in Exodus—Ceremonial

For in six days the Lord made heaven and earth, the sea, and all that in them is, and rested the seventh day; wherefore, the Lord blessed the sabbath day, and hallowed it. (Exodus 20:11)

The reason given in Exodus for the observance of the Sabbath day is that God, in creating, did all the work in six days, and He rested on the seventh and hallowed that day. Therefore, in Exodus the basis is ceremonial or, as we could say today, theological or religious. It is founded upon the fact that God rested on the seventh day.

After Christ had healed the man at the Pool of Bethesda, the religious rulers accused Him of breaking the Mosaic Law because He had done it on the Sabbath day. He said, "My Father worketh hitherto, and I work" (John 5:17). In other words, we are not observing a Sabbath day any longer; we are working!

When we turn to Deuteronomy we find an altogether different reason given for the observance of the Sabbath day.

Basis in Deuteronomy—Humanitarian

Note this passage in Deuteronomy 5:15:

And remember that thou wast a servant in the land of Egypt, and that the Lord thy God brought thee out from there through a mighty hand and by an outstretched arm; therefore the Lord thy God commanded thee to keep the sabbath day.

Back in Exodus the basis is that God rested on the Sabbath, the seventh day, and that basis is theological, ceremonial. But in Deuteronomy we learn that God brought them out of bondage from the land of Egypt, and because of this they were to observe the Sabbath day. They had worked as slaves in hard labor seven days a week, from sunup till sunset, without respite from sorrow or weariness. Now God tells them that, because He has delivered them out of the land of Egypt and permitted them to keep one day of rest, He wants them to be equally considerate of their servants and all their animals. Man and beast must rest one day out of each week. That is human-itarian.

You will recall that our Lord had this in mind when His disciples were plucking the ears of grain on the Sab-bath and the rulers challenged Him because of this. And He said to the religious rulers:

The sabbath was made for man, and not man for the sabbath. (Mark 2:27)

This is a flat statement of the humanitarian aspect of the question. These two reasons are tremendous, and we would do well to keep them in mind.

The Sabbath Belongs to the Hebrews

Since the Sabbath day actually originated in cre-ation—"And on the seventh day God ended his work which he had made; and he rested on the seventh day . . ." (Genesis 2:2)—one would think that all the primitive na-tions of the world would have observed it in some form and at some time. They all did have a garbled account of the Flood and a garbled account of creation, which reveals that there was one reliable source for these. But the interesting thing is that this very important matter of the Sabbath day is not found to be observed by the other nations.

A similar observance in Babylon led liberal scholars to try to trace the Hebrews' observance of the Sabbath back to Babylon. The Babylonians observed the new moon, and there were four quarters in their month. That would work out to seven and sometimes eight days, but it was never Sabbath to them. Dr. R. H. Charles followed the findings of the liberals and their subsequent teachings and made this statement: "The Sabbath belongs to the Hebrews." Isn't that interesting! God had said when He first gave the Law to His people that He wanted them to observe the Sabbath because He had delivered them out of the land of Egypt. Well, who were God's chosen people? I dare say that there are very few reading this book whose ancestors were slaves in Egypt. And even if they were, I have a notion very few of you have ancestors delivered out of the land of Egypt by a mighty act of redemption on God's part. Obviously this applies to a certain group of people who are easily recognized as the nation Israel.

Proofs Pertaining to Israel and the Sabbath

I turn now to several verses in the Word of God which are most significant. First notice Exodus 31:13:

Speak thou also unto the children of Israel [now we know to whom He is speaking]**, saying, Verily my sabbaths ye shall keep; for it is a sign between me and you throughout your generations. . . .**

Here God marked the Sabbath day as a peculiar sign between Himself and the children of Israel.

Then in the next verse God cautioned them further:

Ye shall keep the sabbath therefore; for it is holy unto you: every one that defileth it shall surely be put to death. . . .

That was very serious, was it not? They were to forfeit their very lives for defiling or profaning the Sabbath day.

They were to be dealt with as if they had murdered some-one in cold blood.

Then following through with verses 16 and 17:

Wherefore the children of Israel shall keep the sab-bath, to observe the sabbath throughout their gener-ations, for a perpetual covenant. It is a sign between me and the children of Israel forever. . . .

It is a sign between God and the people of Israel. That is clear, is it not?

Like the rite of circumcision, the Sabbath belongs to the old creation, for the Sabbath was built primarily on the old creation. After God had created during the six days, He rested on the seventh day. Israel, an earthly people, belonged to an old creation, and the Sabbath was given to them as a peculiar sign.

Now if you are not convinced that God meant business about this, turn to another portion in the Book of Num-bers. If you are one who feels that you can keep the Sabbath day and you do keep it, the penalty for breaking it should make your hair stand on end.

In Numbers 15 is an example of one who broke the Sabbath law, beginning with verse 32:

And while the children of Israel were in the wilder-ness, they found a man who gathered sticks upon the sabbath day.

Now I may be wrong, but I have a notion that any one of you readers does more work on the Sabbath or seventh day than this man did. He only picked up a few sticks. Do you want to go under Sabbath day restrictions? Let's go further and learn what happened:

And they who found him gathering sticks brought him unto Moses and Aaron, and unto all the congregation. And they put him in prison, because it was not declared what should be done to him. (vv.33, 34)

We have come now to God's verdict, and it is harsh:

And the LORD said unto Moses, The man shall be surely put to death; all the congregation shall stone him with stones outside the camp. And all the congregation brought him outside the camp, and stoned him with stones, and he died; as the LORD commanded Moses. (vv. 35, 36)

Do you want to be under the law of the Sabbath day? I'm afraid that a great many people who talk of keeping the Sabbath day are breaking it. God meant business about this Sabbath day. Before we conclude this study we shall see the reason God protected the day as He did. We will see that it was symbolic of something tremendous which He has done for you and me. He did not want it violated in any fashion whatever. Neither can you, who talk of keeping the Sabbath, violate what it symbolizes, as we shall see.

Sabbath Day Restrictions

Let us notice some of the things that they could not do on the Sabbath day which the Scripture enjoins. For example, over in Exodus 35:3:

Ye shall kindle no fire throughout your habitations upon the sabbath day.

Now if you were one who kept the Sabbath but you drove your car down to your church on that day, the minute you inserted the key in the ignition and started the motor of your car, you kindled a fire in every one of the cylinders, although you did not see it. In doing this you broke the Sabbath. I called the attention of a friend to this, since he believes he ought to keep the Sabbath. But I notice that he continues to start his car every Saturday, and I see no indication that he is going to start walking. The Jews were forbidden to kindle a fire.

And that's not all of it. I turn again to Exodus and read God's provision for the Sabbath rest during the time He provided manna for His people in the wilderness. Notice this language:

> **And he said unto them, This is that which the LORD hath said, Tomorrow is the rest of the holy sabbath unto the LORD: bake that [manna] which ye will bake today, and boil that ye will boil; and that which remaineth over lay up for you to be kept until the morning. And they laid it up [the leftover manna] till the morning, as Moses bade; and it did not become odious, neither was there any worm in it. And Moses said, Eat that today; for today is a sabbath unto the LORD: today ye shall not find it in the field.** (Exodus 16:23–25)

No cooking was permitted on the Sabbath day at all. And it would not be permissible to go to a restaurant where someone else had done the cooking either.

Exodus 16:29 ties into the above verses:

> **See, the LORD hath given you the sabbath; therefore he giveth you on the sixth day the bread of two days.**

Abide every man in his place, let no man go out on the seventh day.

The expression "a Sabbath day's journey," which is about 750 yards, comes from this verse of Scripture. Therefore the Jews could go no farther than 750 yards on the Sabbath.

When Antiochus Epiphanes made his attack upon the nation Israel, he was able to overcome some of the Maccabees, and the reason was that he attacked on the Sabbath day. He knew that the Jews would not strike back because they would not even engage in defensive warfare on the Sabbath.

When you turn to the Mishnah (or text) which was combined with the commentary in the Talmud (containing the civil and canonical laws of the nation Israel), you will find that they had reduced the Sabbath day observance of Israel to minutiae, the most trifling regulations.

They had thirty-nine ways of breaching the Sabbath, and they divided each one of those thirty-nine ways into another thirty-nine ways, and thirty-nine multiplied by thirty-nine equals 1521 ways in which one could break the Sabbath in Old Testament times!

Let me give you some examples: If you tied a knot you broke the Sabbath. A scribe could not carry a pen because that would be carrying a burden on the Sabbath. A person was not even permitted to kill a flea—it is rather amusing to me that a man could not kill a flea even though it was biting him! In other words, the flea had a free day on the Sabbath. One could not wear a garment or coat that it was possible to carry. The thought was that no coat would be permissible because the person might become too warm, take off his coat and put it over his arm, and that would be carrying a burden on the Sabbath. A woman was not permitted to look in a mirror on the Sabbath day for she might see a gray hair and want to pull it out, and that would be reaping on the Sabbath. Oh, my friend, they had reduced it to where it had become all but ridiculous. Beloved, would you want to revert to the Sabbath?

But we find that God made it very clear to the people of Israel that they were to observe the Sabbath. He said in Leviticus 19:30:

> **Ye shall keep my sabbaths, and reverence my sanctuary: I am the LORD.**

The Sabbath day was bound together with the ceremonial worship of this nation—the two never could be divorced. God said that they must keep holy His Sabbath and His sanctuary.

It is little wonder that Simon Peter stood up in the first Council of Jerusalem and said to those gathered there:

> **Now, therefore, why put God to the test, to put a yoke upon the neck of the disciples [Gentiles], which neither our fathers nor we were able to bear?** (Acts 15:10)

He meant that they, the Jewish people, had not been able to keep all these regulations, so why burden the converted Gentiles with them?

A New Day

When we pass from the Old Testament and come into the New Testament, nothing short of a revolution has taken place as far as the Sabbath day is concerned.

Every commandment is repeated in the Epistles for the Christians as items for our conduct, with one exception—the Sabbath day is not given to Christians. Nowhere is it given to the church. In fact, just the contrary is true, for the church is warned against keeping the Sabbath day, as we shall see.

Our Lord precipitated the wrath of the religious rulers at this very point, and it is here that they broke with Him on the Sabbath question. He claimed to be Lord of the Sabbath, and He justified His claim by raising up the man at the Pool of Bethesda.

My friend, there is one thing that you need to turn over in your mind: Jesus was dead on the Sabbath day! Regardless of what day you think He was crucified, whether it be Wednesday, Thursday or Friday—one thing is obvious, and upon this all agree—He was dead on the Sabbath day.

It was on the first day of the week that He came forth from the dead. And when we turn to the resurrection account in the Gospel of Matthew (which was written primarily to Israel), it opens with a remarkable statement:

In the end of the sabbath, as it began to dawn toward the first day of the week. . . . (Matthew 28:1)

What beautiful language—"In the end of the sabbath"— not just the end of a day, but the end of keeping the Sabbath day, ". . . it began to dawn toward the first day of the week. . . ." That is tremendous!

Pentecost—the Church was Born

Then we turn to the Book of Acts, and there we read that the church was born—and not on a Sabbath day, but the church was born on the Lord's Day, the first day of the week. Notice Acts 2:1:

And when the day of Pentecost was fully come. . . .

What does the Bible mean by "fully come"? Does it mean when the sun had come up or that it was twelve noon or that it was late in the afternoon? No, it does not mean any of that at all. Let me use a parenthesis to make it clear: "When the day of Pentecost [and all of which it spoke] was come. . . ." That which Pentecost had symbolized in the Old Testament is now come. It was the first day of the week, the only first day of the week Israel ever observed—for they observed seven Sabbath days after Passover, and then the day following the seventh Sabbath was Pentecost:

> *On that day the Holy Spirit came.*
> *On that day the church was born.*

Proof that the Church Met on the First Day

It would be exceedingly strange if the church did not make some recognition of the first day of the week. Actually you'll find that the church never met on any day other than the first day of the week. As we turn to Acts 20:7, we find that Paul was preaching in Troas:

And upon the first day of the week, when the disciples came together to break bread, Paul preached unto them, ready to depart on the next day, and continued his speech until midnight.

That was a long sermon! But will you note that the writer

does not insert anywhere such a statement as this, "Now I want to give you a little word of explanation, for it was unusual for the church to meet on the first day of the week." He does not say that for the simple reason that it was the regular time for the church to meet. It can be proven that they never did meet on any other day. There was a group called Ebionites which met on the Sabbath day, but they were called heretics, even by the early church.

Paul said to the Corinthians when he wrote to them:

Upon the first day of the week let every one of you lay by him in store, as God hath prospered him. . . . (1 Corinthians 16:2)

Friends, why should he designate that day? Plainly, that is the day upon which the church came together.

The church is a new creation of God. It belongs not to the old creation; it is a new work:

For by grace are ye saved through faith; and that not of yourselves, it is the gift of God—not of works, lest any man should boast. For we are his workman-ship [his *poeima*, his poem, his creation—a new creation], **created in Christ Jesus unto good works, which God hath before ordained that we should walk in them.** (Ephesians 2:8–10)

And the Christian is a new creation:

Therefore, if any man be in Christ, he is a new creation; old things are passed away; behold, all things are become new. (2 Corinthians 5:17)

Paul writes to the Galatians in the sixth chapter, verse 15:

> **For in Christ Jesus neither circumcision availeth anything, nor uncircumcision, but a new creature [creation].**

John, when on the Isle of Patmos, wrote:

> **I was in the Spirit on the Lord's day.** . . . (Revelation 1:10)

I am aware that a great many commentators hold the position that this has reference to this day of grace in which we live. I will accept that, but I will not rule out the other—it also carries the meaning of the Lord's Day, the first day of the week.

In the opening paragraph of this chapter I made mention of the fact that the Sabbath day has never been changed to Sunday, the first day of the week. A false propaganda has been circulated to the effect that the Roman Catholic Church changed the day of worship from Saturday to Sunday. That needs to be refuted. The church never did observe the Sabbath day; so how could it be changed?

The church observed Sunday, or the Lord's Day, from the beginning. We have this record not only in Acts, but the body of church history also bears testimony to that fact. For example, during the first century we find a lovely thing which corroborates this, a quotation from one of the church fathers, Ignatius, born in A.D. 69 and a disciple of the apostle John:

> No longer observing Sabbaths, but fashioning their lives after the Lord's Day, on which our life also rose through Him.

Also Athanasius, born around A.D. 296, and a great man of the faith, left us this statement:

We keep no Sabbaths: we keep the Lord's Day as a memorial of the beginning of the new creation.

The Epistle of Barnabas, which was never recognized or accepted in the canon of Scripture, though no one has ever questioned the accuracy of its historical statements, contains the following:

I shall make a beginning of the eighth day [that is, Sunday], that is the beginning of another universe. Wherefore we keep also the eighth day [Sunday] for gladness, on which also Jesus rose from the dead.

And the early church always met on the first day of the week to honor and to recognize a resurrected Christ and the fact that they were a new creation. They did not belong to the old creation where the Sabbath day is at the end of the week, but to a new day, the first day of the week.

It may surprise you to learn that the Seventh Day Baptists started the observance of the seventh day, or the sabbath. So you Baptists are going to have to take the blame here. The Presbyterians and the Methodists have already got enough to answer for, and I think that you Baptists ought to shoulder this one. There was a group of people who rose in the early church, the Ebionites. They were called heretics then, and by the sixth and seventh centuries they had called themselves Sabbatarians. It was not until the seventeenth century when Puritan theology became so dominant and legalistic that the Ebionites began to call themselves the Seventh Day

Baptists. And all of the legalists today get the seventh day from them.

The Firm Position of the Lord's Day

Sunday—oh, how important this is to see—does not take the place of Saturday. The Lord's Day is not a substitute for the Old Testament Sabbath day. In fact, all is contrast. C. H. Mackintosh put it this way:

1. The Sabbath was the seventh day; the Lord's Day is the first.
2. The Sabbath was a test of Israel's condition; the Lord's Day is the proof of the church's acceptance, on wholly unconditional grounds.
3. The Sabbath belonged to the old creation; the Lord's Day belongs to the new.
4. The Sabbath was a day of bodily rest for the Jew; the Lord's Day is a day of spiritual rest for the Christian.
5. If the Jew worked on the Sabbath, he was to be put to death. If the Christian does not work on the Lord's Day, he gives little proof of life. That is, if he does not get involved on the Lord's Day in some type of spiritual ministry, he gives little evidence that he has spiritual life. It is a day when you, as a Christian, demonstrate that you belong to Christ. It is not a day when you are to do nothing.

I disagree with those who hold that the Lord's Day is the Sabbath. It is not a Sabbath; it is something new. Today by meeting on the Lord's Day we testify that Jesus came back from the dead. For the early church, every Lord's Day was an Easter! Oh, if we could make every Sunday an Easter—come in our new garments and fill

our churches and talk about the resurrected Christ—
that would be wonderful! Sunday, or the Lord's Day, does
not take the place of Saturday, which is still the Sabbath.

Now I have a suggestion to make. It would be ideal if
we would acknowledge each day as it was intended to be
in its own origin—Saturday, a day of rest, and the Lord's
Day, a day of worship. I believe that the Bible would
sanction that, for it says,

> **One man esteemeth one day above another; another
> esteemeth every day alike. Let every man be fully
> persuaded in his own mind.** (Romans 14:5)

We observe the first day of the week because our Lord
came back from the dead on that day. We do not observe
it as a substitute for the Sabbath day or any other day.

It is vital that we understand that the Sabbath day,
which was part of the ceremonial law, has already been
fulfilled in Christ. And now the injunction given to Christians is clear in Colossians 2:16,17:

> **Let no man, therefore, judge you in food, or in drink,
> or in respect of a feast day, or of the new moon, or of
> a sabbath day: which are a shadow of things to come;
> but the body is of Christ.**

My friend, rituals in the Old Testament were shadows
of things to come, and shadows are photographs. When
a photographer takes our picture, a shadow is registered
on a very sensitive negative. That shadow is developed
and becomes our picture.

The Bible says that as we look back to the Old Testament, we find that even the Sabbath day was a shadow
of something. In the Epistle to the Galatians we find a
tremendously important point:

But now, after ye have known God, or rather are known by God, how turn ye again to the weak and beggarly elements, unto which ye desire again to be in bondage? Ye observe days, and months, and times, and years. (Galatians 4:9, 10)

Beloved, Judaism has passed away, and it says here in Galatians that today it is the same as any other pagan religion. Therefore, to observe the Sabbath in our day is to return to paganism. Such a legal system is one and the same in God's sight!

In coming to the final word in this study, I turn to the Epistle to the Hebrews:

Let us, therefore, fear lest, a promise being left us of entering into his rest, any of you should seem to come short of it. For unto us was the gospel preached, as well as unto them; but the word preached did not profit them, not being mixed with faith in them that heard it. (Hebrews 4:1, 2)

My friend, I keep the Sabbath day—I keep it in accordance with the preceding passage of Scripture.

Now let me give you a personal illustration: When I came to Pasadena to live in 1940, my neighbor, a very fine man but a member of a legalistic system that keeps the seventh day, nailed me first off. I had not been in Southern California twenty-four hours when he buttonholed me and asked, "Do you keep the Sabbath day?" And I looked him right straight in the eye and said, "I sure do." He countered with a gleam in his eye and asked, "What day do you keep?" I looked at him with a gleam in my eye and said to him, "Saturday, Sunday, Monday, Tuesday, Wednesday, Thursday, Friday." And then I started all over again on the next week.

He broke in on my recital and blurted out, "What in the world do you mean?"

I told him something like this: I simply mean that when the Lord Jesus came to this world about two thousand years ago, He said, "My Father worketh hitherto, and I work" (John 5:17).

I tried to make it clear to him that when God had created everything, including man, man sinned and ran into the ditch, and from that day on God did not rest because He wanted to redeem the poor lost sinner and bring him into a place of rest.

On the cross Christ died, but before He died He said to the Father, "It is finished." But when He said it, it was only one word—*Tetelestai!* Finished.

What was finished? The work of redemption was finished so that now you and I can enter into rest. And, my friend, we don't dare try to add any of our good works to His work of redemption! Look again at Ephesians 2:8,9:

For by grace are ye saved through faith; and that not of yourselves, it is the gift of God—not of works, lest any man should boast.

Redemption is a completed package, and He presents it to you wrapped up with everything in it. He doesn't want you to bring your do-it-yourself kit along. He does not need that. When He died on the cross He provided a righteousness that would satisfy a holy God. All He asks of you is to receive this package, this gift of God, which is eternal life in Christ Jesus.

He says, "Come unto me, all ye that labor and are heavy laden, I'll rest you." (Matthew 11:28). In other words, I'll give you a Sabbath in which you can rest in Me, your Savior. He makes every day a Sabbath in which you can rest in Him.

CHAPTER 5

THE FIRST COMMANDMENT WITH A PROMISE
The Fifth Commandment

Honor thy father and thy mother, that thy days may be long upon the land which the LORD thy God giveth thee. (Exodus 20:12)

Since the Ten Commandments are law, they offer no reward or prize for keeping them. On the contrary, a warning is issued that there will be punishment for the breaking of them. And that is true of any law, for that matter. The laws of all lands, the laws of our own country today, bear that similarity. There are no rewards for those who keep the law, and violators are punished.

I drove through the maze of Los Angeles traffic on freeways and streets and highways for two years without getting a traffic ticket, and that was quite a record, I thought. But no representative of our traffic department presented me with a medal or a ribbon or anything else to express their appreciation for my keeping the traffic laws for two years—at least I wasn't caught. But when I was stopped out here in Burbank, the officer didn't feel that it was very much of an argument for me to say that I had not had a ticket in two years.

Well, he was right, because the law offers no rewards whatsoever. The Ten Commandments are couched in foreboding language. They're negative: "Thou shalt not. . . ." They are ominous and threatening.

Some years ago, back East, a church on a corner lot was having trouble with pedestrians cutting across and walking on the grass. Finally the preacher hit upon a novel idea. Because the folk were paying no attention to the sign that read, "Keep off the grass," he replaced it with a sign that read, "Thou shalt not walk on the grass." For some strange reason it worked, and people no longer walked on the grass. But it never has worked for God. The commandments He has given have not been kept.

As we come to the fifth commandment we find something different. It is the exception that proves the rule. It is a commandment that is not negative, a commandment that does not say, "Thou shalt not." Rather, it is couched in positive terms: "Honor thy father and thy mother." Also it offers a reward, ". . . that thy days may be long upon the land which the Lord thy God giveth thee."

Well, in the New Testament Paul the apostle says concerning it that it's the first commandment with a promise. And as far as I know, it's also the last commandment with a promise. In fact, it's the only commandment with a promise. God promised long life to those who would honor their parents. He offered this to His earthly people. By the same token, of course, life was shortened and judgment would follow for those who failed to keep this commandment.

The Bible illustrates this with an example of a prodigal son. You know, there are two prodigal sons in the Bible, one under Mosaic Law (Deuteronomy 21:18-21) and one under Grace (Luke 15:11-32). The Lord Jesus told about the one under Grace because under the Law a prodigal son who was stubborn and rebellious would be brought to the elders of the city, and he would be stoned to death. But in the New Testament our Lord turned that story around and said that when this rebellious son came home, instead of being stoned to death, he was received by his father with open arms and was brought back into a place of sonship.

May I say, that was not Law! Mosaic Law had made it very clear what would happen to the prodigal son. And we find that we don't get very far from the Ten Commandments until God comes back to this matter of the parent/child relationship, and He has some very extreme words to say about it. For instance, in the very next chapter of Exodus, after giving the Ten Commandments, He immediately comes back to this. He says,

And he that smiteth his father, or his mother, shall be surely put to death. . . . And he that curseth his father, or his mother, shall surely be put to death. (Exodus 21:15, 17)

May I say to you, that is extreme. That is severe. That is Law! And that is the way it was under the Mosaic system.

Now in this day in which we live, let me ask this question and then attempt to answer it: How may children honor their parents in accordance with the Scriptures? To begin with, to honor parents means more than yielding obedience in childhood, although it includes that instinctive love and obedience of those early, formative years. But it extends much longer than childhood; in fact, it goes from the cradle to the grave. It means to reverence, it means to respect, it means to express gratitude. All of that is in this command of the Lord to honor your father and your mother.

Now I want us to see three aspects of this commandment that relate to believers today. And, friend, may I make this confession, I'm going to sound as old-fashioned as a celluloid collar, high-button shoes, a kerosene lamp, and an old-fashioned buggy with fringe on the top. Because I'm going back to what God has to say, I'll no doubt make a detour around the modern conception of parent/child relationships. But I have no fear and I offer no apology because I'm on God's side. Martin Luther said, "One with God is a majority," and so I'm in the majority today.

Yielding Obedience in Childhood

Now the first thing I would like to mention concerning honoring father and mother is yielding obedience in childhood. This is the time when children begin to honor their fathers and mothers. The Ten Commandments were divided, and they were divided in an awkward arrangement. That is, four were placed together and six were placed together. The four were man's relationship to God, and the six were man's relationship to man. But it was found that many in the early church did not divide them that way. Tertullian felt that there were five commandments on one table of stone and five commandments on the other, so that they were divided right down the middle and you didn't have the awkward four-six division at all. Also, Canon Frederic Farrar called attention to that, and he said the first five were called *pietas*— that is, man's relationship to God—and then the last five were called *probitas*—man's relationship to man. And Dean Chadwick came along later and made the statement that the fifth commandment was a bridge between these two divisions, and I think probably he's right because the commandment we are looking at in this chapter actually belongs to both sections.

When you say, "Honor your father and your mother," is that man's relationship to God, or is that a man's relationship to his fellow man? I say that it's both. And will you listen to me very carefully? Parents stand in the relationship of God to a young child! I say this reverently, but I say it nonetheless. When a young couple looks down in that crib, and that little, kicking youngster there looks up and squirms and smiles, he's looking at God, as far as the child is concerned!

The parents, to begin with, are like God in that they created that child. The child bears their characteristics. That child is as truly their offspring as Adam was a creation of Almighty God. May I say to you, immediately that ought to alert every parent concerning his responsibility. The mother and father have created someone— that is, brought someone into this world—and that establishes a different relationship. The child looks instinctively, in love and faith, to the parent as he looks to no one else. When he is brought up in that home with those parents, that little one's life begins to look to his parents, and they occupy the place of God. All the love and all the faith of that little one is placed in the parents.

I remember an incident that illustrates this in my own experience right at the end of World War II, when we could drive freely again because gas was no longer rationed. My family and I were coming back from Texas and came into Yuma, Arizona, rather late in the evening. But Yuma was the staging center during the war and was then the place where men were being released from the service, so that every motel and every hotel was filled. We crossed over the Colorado River and naturally had to go by the inspection station for California. That was the first time that I ever felt kindly toward a checking station as I was coming into my home state. The man there was very courteous, and he let my wife take our little one inside where it was warm and give her a bottle in there. Then when we got back into the car we bedded her down between us. I never shall forget driving practically all that night on the highway, where it was filled with military trucks—a rather dangerous situation— how she just went right to sleep. I'd look down at her as I was driving and think, *My, what faith she has in her daddy, to drive her tonight.* But she had that faith. And as I rode along, I learned something for my own heart and life, and I lifted a silent prayer, "O God, if I only had that faith in You! When it's dangerous and the going looks rough, if I could only go right off to sleep and just leave it to You and trust You." What a wonderful thing it would be.

May I say that a parent is in a unique position in the life of a child. That child is dependent upon the parent for everything. The Word of God even sends the little one to the parents to be taught. God says to the boy, "My son, hear the instruction of thy father, and forsake not the law of thy mother" (Proverbs 1:8). God says that!

This puts a tremendous responsibility on parents. If parents fulfill their God-appointed task and they honor God in their lives and are genuine in the home, that child normally will transfer his reverence and his faith to God when he reaches the age when he is bound to discover that his parents have feet of clay, that they're not as perfect as he thought they were. There will be no serious gap at that time because normally the little one will look away to God in that same simple faith with which he looked in the beginning to the parents. That's not harsh; that's God's gracious provision for the little ones.

You do a child an injustice when you do not discipline him and make him obedient to you, for the very simple reason that it is God's intention, during those formative and impressionable years, that the little one should play and be free of responsibility and free from making decisions. He lives in his little world of discovery and make-believe, where his little mind and heart and body are being developed. It is the time for fun, and believe me, if that little one's going to have to make his own decisions, if he's not going to be obedient, he's going to lose a lot of his fun. Childhood is a time of laughter, a time of great activity, when he needs to be curbed.

I saw a cartoon several years ago, and I still chuckle when I think of it. There was a picture of a market with all kinds of breakfast food on the shelves, and this mother had come in. She had a little fellow by the hand, and you could tell that he was full of vim, vigor and vitality—my, he was an active-looking youngster! But she was wan and worn. Her hair was disheveled and she had a bedraggled look. She said to the cashier there at the counter, "Do you have anything that is the opposite of Wheaties?" May I say to you, she'd already had fourteen rounds—and she was knocked out in the fifteenth round.

However, it's God's intention during the early years that the little one shall be obedient to the parents—for the sake of the child. Because, if the child doesn't obey, he'll become unhappy. Do you know that the unhappiest children you find today are those children who come out of homes where they have not been made to obey? They are the unhappiest bunch of brats you'll ever meet. And disobedience will lead, later on, to a wrecked life. It always does, my beloved. Therefore, in God's Word is this gracious provision for the little one:

My son, hear the instruction of thy father, and forsake not the law of thy mother. (Proverbs 1:8)

And then, when you come over to the New Testament, you find that He hasn't changed His law. This is for you and for me as believers today:

Children, obey your parents in the Lord; for this is right. (Ephesians 6:1)

Does this mean that the parents are in the Lord or that the children are in the Lord here? Personally, I think it means both because I don't think that any child can honor a parent who is not worthy to be honored, and I'm not sure God has asked a child to honor a parent who is unworthy of honor.

I knew a young fellow, a schoolmate in college, whose father was a drunkard. His point was this: "I always want to honor the man that I wanted my dad to be." May I say, that was, I think, the healthy and the Christian outlook God intended for him to have.

Now God is very insistent on this for believers. If you turn over to Colossians 3:20, you'll find something that's quite interesting. Again Paul comes back to the subject. He says,

Children, obey your parents in all things; for this is well-pleasing unto the Lord.

This is Christian conduct in the home.

Now, my beloved, we need to note that every commandment of the Ten Commandments is repeated in the Epistles for believers, with the one exception of the fourth, regarding the Sabbath day. That is the one that was *not* given to the church, but the other nine were given to us, and this one is definitely for believers: "Honor thy father and mother (which is the first commandment with promise)," and then He makes this statement, "that it may be well with thee, and thou mayest live long on the earth" (Ephesians 6:2,3). Now you will notice that those last three words, "on the earth," indicate a new location, and rightly so, because back in the Old Testament God said to the people of Israel, "You are to honor your father and mother that you might live long in the land which the Lord thy God giveth thee." That land was Israel, and I'm confident that God hasn't promised long life in the land of Israel to any of us today. It looks like no one is going to have safe living over there, certainly not in these days. But back in the Old Testament God promised to His people long life in the Promised Land if they kept this commandment. Now in the New Testament God's promise is long life "on the earth," and that would include wherever you live today. So this commandment is for you and me.

Now will you notice, the New Testament has added something more to it for us in our day. In the next verse we read,

And, ye fathers, provoke not your children to wrath, but bring them up in the nurture and admonition of the Lord. (Ephesians 6:4)

This is a section for parents, and it is so important that God repeated it over in Colossians 3:21:

Fathers, provoke not your children to anger, lest they be discouraged.

And today God says to us that the child whom He has given us is not a creature to vent our temper upon. The child is not to be ordered around as a slave. He is not to be a pawn of the feelings of the parents. He is not to be used to indulge the whim of the parent at all. How often Proverbs 22:6 has been misinterpreted as, "Bring up or train up a child in the way he should go and, when he is old, he will not depart from it." Well, if you'll look at it very carefully in the Hebrew, you'll find that God doesn't mean the way the parents want him to go. The literal language there is this: "Bring up a child *in his way*," which means that God has a way for every child to go, and it's up to the parents to find out what that way is. The parents, by walking with God, can find out how God wants them to bring up the little one. And the New Testament makes it very clear that discipline and instruction go with it, for the word *nurture* here means "discipline," and *admonition* here means "instruction." Raise your child in the nurture and the admonition, or the discipline and the instruction, of the Lord.

Believe me, friend, here is the place today where modern education has broken down completely. Every now and then I notice there's supposedly a change in the schools—back to the three Rs. Johnny is to buckle down to reading, writing and arithmetic—and discipline—after years of progressive education. May I say to you, I always hope that it's true. I'm sorry, but I am skeptical. I'm going to have to see it myself to believe it, but if there is such a trend, it's a trend back to God's viewpoint.

I wonder if you've ever noticed what God says concerning this matter of discipline in the home. Will you listen to Him, and I'll quote from the Amplified Bible which couches it in more understandable language for us today:

Withhold not discipline from the child, for if thou strike and punish him with the [reed-like] rod, he will not die. (Proverbs 23:13)

My mother would paddle me when I was a boy, and to get off easy, my method was to yell at the top of my voice, "You're killing me! You're killing me!" and she would let up. God says in effect, "Go ahead and lay it on, he won't die. It will be the best thing in the world for him."

It was good for me, and I do believe that it is still good today.

Start your discipline when your children are young. Don't wait until it is too late. A man who was saved later in life told me, "My wife and I were saved recently, and we are thanking God for it, but we have lost our children. We used to live like the devil, and we can see that in our children today." They had waited until too late to give their children the proper training.

Start when the children are young. Don't mind if little Willie cries when you paddle him. On the other hand, every father needs to be very careful in the way he deals with his child. No one has the right to be brutal in his dealings with his children. Dr. Ironside has translated the proverb this way: "Chasten thy son while there is hope, but set not thy soul upon slaying him." Don't be afraid to discipline, but a brutal punishment is not to be permitted. Brutality can only tear down the child and destroy his spirit. As a matter of fact, even the law of the land can, and should, step in whenever there is brutality to children.

God has given very definite commands for Christians. He tells children to obey their parents (Ephesians 6:1). But then he says to the fathers, "And, ye fathers, provoke not your children to wrath . . ." (Ephesians 6:4). Don't wade into them when you are angry. They know you are angry and that you are just venting your anger and frustration. At that time you will probably punish too hard—in fact, you can be brutal. The command is to bring them up in the ". . . nurture and admonition of the Lord" (Ephesians 6:4)—that is, the discipline and the instruction of the Lord.

But may I say this to you, insubordination in the home leads to recklessness. And that is what God says. When you honor your father and mother you'll be given long life. This is a natural law, because the person who has learned to honor his father and mother by obedience in the home grows up to be a stable individual. If he has been living a life of insubordination, he moves out into the world and recklessness characterizes his life. My beloved, I say this kindly, all of this rebelliousness, irresponsible behavior and gang activity is a result of a lack of discipline in the home. Usually parents are to blame. It's too bad that instead of arresting these boys and girls, police can't go and arrest the guilty parents. I believe that many parents will stand before the judgment bar of God as the murderers of their own children, having permitted them to grow up in insubordination. And I tell you, you can't use alcohol or drugs and race at seventy miles an hour on our city streets without getting into a great deal of difficulty. And lack of discipline in the home is the thing that leads to it.

Actually, juvenile delinquency is usually parental delinquency. Have you ever noticed in the Old Testament the number of men who were God's men, wonderful men, but were failures as fathers? And this ought to cause all of us who are in Christian work today—ministers and missionaries included—to search our hearts.

Let's look at a few examples and begin with the man by the name of Aaron, God's first high priest. Have you ever read in Leviticus 10:1-3 the story of how his two eldest sons, Nadab and Abihu, rebelled against God and how the fire of the Lord came out and destroyed them? And I've always been interested in Aaron's conduct. It says there, "And Aaron held his peace." He had nothing to say. Aaron couldn't go into God's presence and say, "O God, why did You do this?" Aaron knew it had been failure on his part, and Aaron held his peace.

Eli, in the tradition of Aaron, a high priest in Israel— he's the one who trained little Samuel, by the way—is another example of a permissive father. It was said of his sons in 1 Samuel 2:12, they were "sons of Belial"—that is, sons of the devil. They were lost. From Aaron to Eli, there had been failures in the home, and God then took away the influence of the high priest.

Samuel, great man that he was, when you read his story you find out that his boys got away from God (cf 1 Samuel 8:1–5), and what a failure he was as a father!

And then David, the best king that Israel ever had and a man who had a heart for God, was a sorry failure as a father. David had many sons, but he loved one boy above all his other children. His name was Absalom.

Apparently David wanted Absalom to be king after him rather than Solomon. He *didn't* want Solomon on the throne because, in my opinion, he thought he was a sissy. Read in 1 Kings 2 his instructions to that boy. He said to him on his deathbed, "Solomon, be strong and show yourself a man." In other words, "You've been brought up here in the women's palace; you don't know what hardship really is. Now play the man!"

David's son Absalom was the one he had loved, but he had spoiled him. Oh, how he spoiled Absalom. And Absalom was slain when he rebelled against his father. It broke David's heart. Personally, I don't think David ever recovered from that. When word came to him of Absalom's death, he took his great cloak and covered his head.

And the king was much moved, and went up to the chamber over the gate, and wept; and as he went, thus he said, O my son Absalom, my son, my son Absalom! Would God I had died for thee, O Absalom, my son, my son! (2 Samuel 18:33)

He knew that Absalom was lost, and he would have taken his place—oh, he would have taken his place so gladly.

My beloved, may I say, the failures of Eli, Samuel and David are lessons to those of us who are fathers in places of Christian leadership relative to our own children.

Now let's look at something that is so very different. When we come to the New Testament, our Lord Jesus becomes an example to us. You remember the one incident when He was twelve years of age, recorded in Luke, chapter 2. I think that is the loveliest story. You remember that they were in Jerusalem at the feast, and when Mary and Joseph left there that day, Jesus did not go, and later His parents missed Him. So many criticize Mary for carelessness. My friend, don't you know that when Mary was so agitated that afternoon, the reason was that Jesus had never been out of her sight before? Think of that. For twelve years she kept her eye on that boy. God knew what He was doing when He made her the mother. What a rebuke again to those of us in Christian service. Personally, I do not believe that any parents have the right to turn over the training of their children to someone else. That is our responsibility, and too many of us in Christian work are away from home so much. Oh, my friend, Mary had never let Him get out of her sight before. Now He was gone, and she went back and found Him. He wasn't rebuking her when He said, "How is it that ye sought me? Knew ye not that I must be about my Father's business?" In other words, "Mother mine, I've been here. You've taught Me these things, and don't you know I must be about My Father's business?"

But then I read this startling thing. The record states that He went down with them to Nazareth, and He was *subject* unto them. Let me see you crawl out from under that! The Lord of Glory in His humanity went down to Nazareth at twelve years of age, and He was subject to Mary and Joseph!

Then many years later I find Him, when He begins His

ministry, doing a strange thing that has blessed my heart as I've been reading in the Gospel of Mark (3:31–35). You remember that one time He was teaching His apostles, and from outside the word came that "Your mother and Your brothers are looking for You." And He said a very strange thing. To paraphrase, "Who is My mother or My brothers?" Then looking at the multitude sitting around Him, He said, "Behold, My mother and My brothers!" Then He went on, "Whoever does the will of God is My brother, and My sister, and mother." Oh, how wonderful that is. What He's saying is this: "I've passed the period now of obedience, and the greatest relationship that I've had in this world has been with Mary and My half-brothers and half-sisters yonder in Nazareth. But now there is a greater relationship, and that relationship is here." In other words, "If you come to Me and do the will of the Father, you're the ones who are closer to Me than even My blood relatives." He is saying now that there is something higher and holier even than a family relationship, and that is when a person, a sinner in rebellion against God, comes in *obedience* by simple faith in Christ. In yielding obedience to Him, by trusting Him, a new relationship is established which is the highest relationship this world knows anything about, even above parent and child.

Expressing Gratitude As Adults

As adults, we honor our parents when we express gratitude to them. A very wonderful thing is said by Paul as he is writing to Timothy, this young preacher, and giving instructions,

But if any widow have children or nephews, let them learn first to show piety at home, and to requite their parents; for that is good and acceptable before God. (1 Timothy 5:4)

Paul says that children are to "requite their parents," and that doesn't mean to keep them quiet. However, it has been translated by some children to mean that. But it does mean to *repay* them. It means to show *gratitude*. It means to express to them our appreciation, and we honor them when we express it.

There is a time that comes in a person's life when he no longer obeys—it would be wrong if he did obey. It is tragic today to see young adults tied to their mama's apron strings when they ought to be out on their own in the world. But when that young person moves out in the world, he needs to express his gratitude to his parents. Have you ever stopped to think how many diapers your mama washed for you? Have you ever thought of her sleepless nights when she cared for you during illness? Suppose you paid her what you pay a baby-sitter today— she would be a millionaire!

Have you ever stopped to think of how your father worked and sacrificed to send you to college? Someone has said that the college-bred man is a four-year loaf made out of father's dough. And believe me, my friend, there's many a one just like that today. It was Shakespeare's King Lear who said, and he knew from experience, "How sharper than a serpent's tooth it is to have a thankless child." We dishonor our parents when we neglect them. I'm so glad to see the missions and these service centers putting up the sign again, "Have you written home to mother?" I know it sounds sentimental, but have *you* written home to your mother lately? Or are you neglecting your father and mother? I don't care how active you are in Christian service, you cannot convey the precepts God wants to set forth if you dishonor your parents.

Showing Respect Throughout Life

And then let me say this, that we honor our parents by showing respect to them during the total span of their lives. This is the thing, you will recall, the writer of Proverbs said:

Hearken unto thy father that begot thee, and despise not thy mother when she is old. (Proverbs 23:22)

I'd like to add this: you will always be the child of your parents although you may live to be a hundred years old. Even Methuselah was always a son of Enoch, and I often think of him, not as the old man with the cane, but as the little baby in a crib the day his dad Enoch walked in and looked down at him. And when Enoch saw him, the Word of God says,

And Enoch walked with God after he begot Methuselah three hundred years, and begot sons and daughters. And all the days of Enoch were three hundred sixty and five years. And Enoch walked with God, and he was not; for God took him. (Genesis 5:22–24)

From that day on he walked with God. And when Methuselah was 969 years old, he was still the son of Enoch. You will reveal to your dying day the instructions and the discipline that you received in your childhood.

My friend, by the same token you can turn this around, and parents today can claim their children for God. I believe that any child who has gone astray from God and is away from God right now, if that child was brought up in the discipline and instruction of the Lord, the parent can claim that child for God, and God is bound to hear and answer. Let me put it a different way. God will hear and answer that prayer.

I remember hearing Dr. Peter Philpott in Los Angeles many years ago. It was the first time I ever heard him speak, and I'll never forget the message. He told a story that came out of his first pastorate in a church in Ohio. In that little church was a very godly man and he was the leading deacon. Dr. Philpott said that the little church didn't pay the pastor too much in those days, and when he got behind, this deacon would always write out a personal check and say, "Don't tell anybody about it." He was that type of person, a godly man, one you could depend on.

The man's wife had died, and his sons were gone, one living in Chicago and the other living in Pittsburgh. But this man had a heartbreak. His son in Chicago was a Christian, he was sure, but his son in Pittsburgh he was sure was not a Christian. Dr. Philpott said that he went over to visit this deacon a great deal and that every time he would go over there, before leaving they would have prayer together. The father would always say, "Be sure and remember to pray for my boy in Pittsburgh, that God will save him."

This old man died, and the two sons came to the funeral. It was the first time Dr. Philpott, as a young preacher, had the opportunity of meeting them. Before the old man died, he had said to Dr. Philpott, "When you preach at my funeral, preach to my boy from Pittsburgh. Give him the gospel—oh, give him the gospel. Tell him what I believe, and let him know I want him to be saved."

And Dr. Philpott said, "You know, that's what I did. I preached to that boy at the funeral."

The funeral was held on Saturday, and it was a very sad occasion for the entire community. But since it took so much of his Saturday, Dr. Philpott hadn't gotten up his sermons for Sunday. Believe me, he had to dig, so he went to the church and upstairs to his study. Along about seven or eight o'clock he heard a knock on the door and went down to answer it. There was the boy from Chicago. He said, "I'm taking the train in just a few moments, but I wanted to come by and thank you for conducting the funeral and for the things that you said. And I want you to know that I had gotten away from God, but I'm coming back to Him, you can be sure of that." Then he went on out to catch his train.

It was nearly midnight, but Dr. Philpott was still working on his sermons when there was another rap at the door. He went down the stairs again, and it was the other boy, the son from Pittsburgh, who was then a very wealthy man. He came up to his study and said, "I've come by to tell you that Dad's contribution to this church will continue as long as I live. And I want to hand you something, because I know *he* would do it." And he gave him a check. Then the man looked like he had something else to say. He started to go, then turned and said, "Maybe I should tell you this because I know you were speaking to me this afternoon. I've been over to the old home place, and it brought back a lot of memories of my mom and my dad. As I walked through the house, I could almost see them. I went into my dad's room, and there was that rocking chair that you saw him in so often. I stood there, and I honestly believe I felt his presence. As I looked at that old rocking chair, I knew that he had knelt there for hours, praying for me. And," he paused for a moment, "before I got out of that room, I went and knelt down at that rocking chair, and I took Christ as my Savior." He added, "I thought maybe you'd like to know it."

This father went to glory without seeing his boy come to Christ, but he had faith that he would come!

Beloved, God sends the little ones to the parents to be taught. He says to the children, "My son, hear the instruction of thy father, and do not forsake the law of thy mother" (Proverbs 1:8, KJV). And then He says to the parents, ". . . You fathers, don't provoke your children to anger, but bring them up in the discipline and instruction of the Lord" (Ephesians 6:4). And to all of us He says, "Honor your father and mother, which is the first commandment with promise . . ." (Ephesians 6:2).

CHAPTER 6

MURDER
The Sixth Commandment

Thou shalt not kill. (Exodus 20:13)

"Thou shalt not kill," or more accurately, "Thou shalt not murder," is the sixth of the Ten Commandments which were engraved by God Himself on tablets of stone and given to the people of Israel.

Do they have any relevance for our lives today? Absolutely! They are God's expressed will for all mankind, and they reveal to us that we fall short of the glory of God. Regardless of current philosophies to the contrary, God has given to the entire human family His standard for right and wrong. Past civilizations which have violated His laws have disappeared from the face of the earth and lie this moment in rubble and ashes.

Now when we begin to inspect this commandment we find there are other complications that are connected with it. It is not so simple. The fact of the matter is that this is the most complicated commandment of all. This fact is illustrated by two news stories that are in the headlines at the time of this writing. One involves a Methodist preacher, riding with a friend, an officer of the law and, I suppose, a member of his church, on the officer's day off. Suddenly their holiday was interrupted by a special bulletin coming in over the radio, ordering this officer by name to a roadblock. He went there, and unfortunately the criminal came that way. The officer, when he attempted to stop the criminal, was shot down in cold blood. Then the criminal attempted to shoot this preacher, but the preacher was very quick on the draw. He got a gun that was in the car and he killed the criminal. Now the question is, was this preacher justified in shooting the criminal? Did he break the sixth commandment?

The second news item concerns a state governor who was out in the bay on a battleship. A criminal had been convicted and sentenced to die in the gas chamber. At the last moment an attorney for the criminal had made a hurried telephone call to the battleship asking the governor for a reprieve. Then a call from the battleship went back to the land. The stage had evidently been set, and those who participated certainly did ham it up. It was as thrilling as a "whodunit" and dramatized the battle against capital punishment. "Is capital punishment a relic of a barbaric age?" questioned one newspaper columnist.

These cases reveal some of the complications that are connected with the sixth commandment. On the surface it may seem very simple, but to understand what God had in mind, it will be necessary for us to dissect it and give it some study. Briefly, we will deal with the intrinsic value of the sixth commandment, the inherent nature of the sixth commandment, and then the indispensable necessity for the sixth commandment, even in this day in which we live.

Intrinsic Value

To alert you to the intrinsic value of the sixth commandment, let me make a rather startling statement: The sixth commandment is the most important and vital commandment to you and your family and to every person on the topside of this earth. The sixth commandment is basic to all human governments. It's the foundation of contemporary society. It is the bulwark of all civilization.

The violation of this commandment was the first outbreak of sin after man disobeyed God in the Garden of Eden. It was the murder by Cain of his brother Abel, recorded in Genesis 4:8. Then God's pronouncement of Cain's punishment is in verses 11-13:

And now art thou cursed from the earth, which hath opened her mouth to receive thy brother's blood from thy hand; when thou tillest the ground, it shall not henceforth yield unto thee its strength; a fugitive and a wanderer shalt thou be in the earth. And Cain said unto the LORD, My punishment is greater than I can bear.

That's interesting. At the very beginning, the first sinner who committed this overt act of murder said his punishment was greater than he could bear—and that was true. It is unfortunate that Cain did not turn to a substitute and receive forgiveness—God would have provided a substitute. But Cain attempted to bear, in his own body, the punishment for his sin. And yet, God forbade that any man should put his hand on Cain because of this crime. God put around him a hedge and said that no man could touch him. That seems exceedingly strange.

But when you turn a few pages of the Scriptures and you come to the time of Noah after the Flood, you find that the human family has moved into an altogether different era. The first great civilization upon the earth had been washed out in the Flood. Those who came through that devastation to the other side were Noah and his family. After the Flood not only do we have a new beginning for the human race, but we find God putting man on a different foundation altogether—a foundation that was different from that which gave protection even to a murderer. However, even before the Flood, the murderer had to bear his own punishment.

Turning now to the ninth chapter of Genesis, we read God's instructions to Noah after the Flood:

> **And surely your blood of your lives will I require; at the hand of every beast will I require it, and at the hand of man; at the hand of every man's brother will I require the life of man. Whoso sheddeth man's blood, by man shall his blood be shed; for in the image of God made he man.** (vv. 5, 6)

This was the institution of capital punishment, and it was put for the first time into the hands of man. When a man's life is taken, in that which (as we shall see) is murder, then the murderer is to have his life taken in turn.

That command was never repealed, it never has been revoked; it is the foundation of all government. It was given to protect human life, and I do think that we need to see how important it is.

Why should not human life be taken? Well, may I say to you that the reasons advanced today are not biblical reasons. I have noticed that several criminals, right before their executions, have made this kind of statement, "I'm paying my debt to society." Also you hear it said, "This crime is so heinous, so terrible, that the one who perpetrated it should pay." May I say to you that neither view is the basis of capital punishment according to the Word of God. Neither is capital punishment to be enforced in the spirit of revenge. It is not an idea of getting even. It is not the government, as a big Shylock, demanding its pound of flesh. And, my friend, it is not even the cold justice of "eye for eye, and tooth for tooth." None of these is the basis of capital punishment.

You may say, "Those are the reasons that are given to us today. Can there be any other reason?" Yes. God gives it here:

> **Whoso sheddeth man's blood, by man shall his blood be shed; for in the image of God made he man.** (Genesis 9:6)

Why is human life sacred? I'll tell you why. Man has been made in the image of God—this is the only thing that makes human life sacred. If man is an animal in the process of evolution, then life is not sacred. Over a century of that kind of teaching has produced the greatest crime wave in what is probably the most enlightened nation in the world's history. Oh, if we could only get back to God's basis! God's basis is that since He created man in His image, there should be a reverence for human life. My friend, when you strike at a human being it is an indirect way of striking at God, because that person is in the image of God—defaced by sin though he may be. Man in the image of God is the only thing that makes life sacred today. It is the only thing that gives value to it. That is the intrinsic value of this law; it is the basis of it. Because man is in God's image, you and I dare not take human life.

Does this apply to abortion? Let's look at Psalms 139:13-16:

> **For thou hast possessed [formed] my inward parts; thou hast covered me in my mother's womb.** (v. 13)

From the time we are conceived in the womb, we never get away from the presence of God in this life.

He reinforces this truth in the next verse:

I will praise thee; for I am fearfully and wonderfully made. Marvelous are thy works, and that my soul knoweth right well. (v. 14)

God is everywhere, and each person is a fabulous creature who has the attention of God constantly.

My substance was not hidden from thee, when I was made in secret, and intricately wrought in the lowest parts of the earth. Thine eyes did see my substance, yet being unformed; and in thy book all my members were written, which in continuance were fashioned, when as yet there was none of them. (vv. 15, 16)

Before his body was formed David says he was a person. He was a person as he was being formed (literally, skillfully woven) in the womb. The personhood is declared to take place at the very moment of conception.

This is very important in our day because of the question of abortion. I heard a minister of the liberal persuasion say that the Bible has nothing to say about abortion and therefore we can make our own decision or do as we please. However, the Bible does have something to say about it, and here is a clear-cut reference. While the body was being formed, David said he was a person, a human being. God had the blueprint of his members before they came into existence! The person was there.

Now hear it straight: abortion is murder unless it is performed to save the mother's life. Abortion to get rid of the little unformed fellow before he has an opportunity to utter a cry is murder. Doing it in order to cover up sin or escape responsibility merely enhances the awful and cruel crime. Do not blame me for this charge. Blame David—he wrote it. Blame God—He declared it.

Now notice this distinction: it is not human life *ipso facto*, that is, the life in itself that is sacred, because in God's economy there have been martyrs who have sacrificed their lives—thrown them away and poured them out like water. They did not count them sacred. The writer to the Hebrews says of that great company, ". . . And others were tortured, not accepting deliverance . . ." (Hebrews 11:35).

How we need that dedication of human life to God in this day, a dedication that means something—not just attending services on Sunday, or serving on a committee, or rendering some little service to Him. We need the whole life dedicated on the altar to God! I tell you, that's the only thing the world outside will be impressed by, my beloved. It's not our doctrine that will impress the world; it is our dedication. And how we need that today! Life is not sacred in and of itself.

There is a mystery about life. You cannot give it, and, my friend, you have no right to take it. Only God can give life, and since only God can give life, He alone has the right to take it, or it can be taken only according to His specific law. No one else has that right.

Othello, in Shakespeare's play, when he went in to murder his wife Desdemona, found a light burning on the table beside her. He made a play upon the two "lights"—the light that was there in the candle and the one that was in her body, the light of life. And he said this:

> *Put out the light, and then put out the light.*
> *If I quench thee, thou flaming minister,*
> *I can again thy former light restore,*

Should I repent me: but once put out thy light,
Thou cunning'st pattern of excelling nature,
I know not where is that Promethean heat
That can thy light relume.

That was the thing that held back his hand for awhile. He wondered if he dare take her life because he could not put it back. But the light on the candle he could blow out, and if he had made a mistake, he could relight it. He could not restore human life. There is a mystery about it, and for that reason, God says it is sacred.

Let me inject here an opinion. I think that it ought to be illegal to have all these showings of killings on television and in movies. I think it is without doubt one of the most dangerous things because it treats human life as something cheap, certainly not in the image of Almighty God! Man's creation in the image of God is the reason human life is not to be taken.

Inherent Nature

Second, we must take into consideration the inherent nature of the sixth commandment, "Thou shalt not murder." Here is a place where some of the newer translations missed an opportunity to make a needed improvement over the way we find it in the Authorized Version. The New King James translates it, "You shall not murder." That is much more accurate than "Thou shalt not kill," because it is possible to kill without murdering. There is a cult today that accepts the Ten Commandments but rejects the remainder of the Mosaic Law. That is perfectly absurd. You need all the Mosaic Law to interpret the Ten Commandments, and that is especially true of the sixth commandment, because there are degrees of murder: first degree, justifiable homicide, manslaughter, self-defense—and the Scriptures recognize all of these. There are ten Hebrew words translated by our English word "kill." In Exodus 20:13, the Hebrew word is *ratsach*, which means "murder."

Now I want to call your attention to these distinctions that are made in the Mosaic Law concerning the sixth commandment, "Thou shalt not murder." Over in Exodus 21 which, by the way, immediately follows the giving of the Ten Commandments, we have set before us that which is first degree murder.

He that smiteth a man, so that he die, shall be surely put to death. (v. 12)

This is first degree murder. And here it is premeditated murder:

But if a man come presumptuously upon his neighbor, to slay him with guile, thou shalt take him from mine altar, that he may die. (Exodus 21:14)

God is saying that if a man plans and plots the murder of another, he shall be taken even if he goes in to the altar and lays hold of the horns of the altar, which always signified a cry for mercy. God says that such a man shall not have mercy; he shall be put to death. That is first degree murder of the very worst sort.

Now will you notice, even God puts down the penalty for attempted murder:

And if men strive together, and one smite another with a stone, or with his fist, and he die not, but keepeth his bed; if he rise again, and walk abroad upon his staff, then shall he that smote him be clear:

**only he shall pay for the loss of his time, and shall
cause him to be thoroughly healed.** (Exodus 21:18,
19)

That is attempted murder. And a man was not to die for
attempted murder. But he was to pay his victim's medical
expenses and the time he lost while recuperating.

Now we come to a most unusual arrangement. That's
the interesting thing about God's arrangements—they're
unusual and not always according to man's way of doing
things. This next law was to protect those who had killed
innocently; that is, those guilty of manslaughter. They
may have been negligent, other things may have entered
in, but God gave them a protection. There are several
passages that deal with this, but I'll use the one in Deuteronomy:

**Thou shalt set apart three cities. . . . Thou shalt
prepare thee a way, and divide the borders of thy
land, which the Lord thy God giveth thee to inherit,
into three parts, that every slayer may flee there. . . .
And if the Lord thy God enlarge thy borders. . . then
shalt thou add three cities more beside these three,
that innocent blood be not shed in thy land. . . .**
(Deuteronomy 19:2, 3, 8–10)

In other words, God appointed six cities of refuge in
the land of Israel, three on one side of the Jordan River
and three on the other side, designated places on both
the east and west banks of the Jordan River. These cities
were arranged geographically so that a person in any
part of the land was able to get to one quickly. The purpose for these cities of refuge was for the protection of
a person who would slay another accidentally, yet some
relative, or even a mob, might feel he had done it pur-

posely and would try to do away with him. He could flee
to a city of refuge where he would be safe. The cities, by
the way, were the Levites' cities. The man was to be
brought before the Levites, God's priests, and was to be
given an opportunity to state his case. If it was determined that he had done it accidentally, then this man
could stay inside the city of refuge and no one could
harm him.

He gives a practical illustration lifted out of life in
Israel of that day:

> **And this is the case of the slayer who shall flee there,
> that he may live: whoso killeth his neighbor uninten-
> tionally, whom he hated not in time past; [**and now
> he gives an illustration**] as when a man goeth into
> the forest with his neighbor to hew wood, and his
> hand swingeth with the axe to cut down the tree,
> and the head slippeth from the helve and lighteth
> upon his neighbor, that he die; he shall flee unto one
> of those cities, and live.** (Deuteronomy 19:4, 5)

This gets right down where people lived. Suppose two
men go out into the woods to cut down trees to build a
house. As one man is swinging his axe, the head slips off
the handle and strikes the other man in the temple and
kills him instantly. When he realizes what has happened,
he is afraid to go report it in the city where they live
because he knows that this man's brother is a hotheaded
fellow who doesn't like him anyway, and he has a notion
that he will think he did it purposely. So this man goes
immediately to the closest city of refuge where he cannot
be touched. He will be safe (as long as he stays inside
the city limits) until he can be given a fair trial without
any prejudice and without any heat. Now that was God's

wonderful arrangement to take care of this type of thing that would come up in Israel.

There were many other things for which men were held guilty of murder. For instance this,

And he that smiteth his father, or his mother, shall be surely put to death. (Exodus 21:15)

By inference and interpretation of the law, I think there were many additional things for which capital punishment was required. I'll mention a few, with no attempt to prove them by Scripture, hoping you will follow them through in the Bible. Sons or daughters who left home, went off into sin and broke their parents' hearts so that they died, in God's sight were guilty of murder. If a man betrayed a girl, and that girl, finding that she was to be disgraced, took her own life, the man was guilty of murder in God's sight. Also abortion is murder in God's sight. And the drunk driver who gets into a car, drives down the highway and kills someone, is a murderer in God's sight.

I believe Scripture infers that the men who made the liquor and sold it to him are guilty of murder also. I take it that the laws relating to man's responsibility to man would cover that situation because God gives the following example of a certain restriction on building permits:

When thou buildest a new house, then thou shalt make a parapet for thy roof, that thou bring not blood upon thine house, if any man fall from there. (Deuteronomy 22:8)

You see how this operated. A man built a house and didn't put a railing or parapet around the roof, which was the front porch or patio in that day. If anyone fell off and broke his neck, the man who built that house was guilty of murder. God, you see, makes us responsible for safeguarding the lives of our fellowmen.

Even a person who has a malicious tongue and plunges it like a knife into the back of another person's character—this one is also considered a murderer in God's sight.

This law has many ramifications.

Indispensable Necessity

As we have been considering this sixth commandment, we have seen its intrinsic value, its inherent nature, and now we will see the indispensable necessity of the commandment, "Thou shalt not murder."

When we get to the New Testament, we find that this commandment was not repealed or revoked. All the Ten Commandments are repeated for Christians, with the exception of the one regarding the Sabbath day. The sixth commandment, "Thou shalt not murder," is given in the New Testament, and our Lord did something remarkable to it. He lifted it to the nth degree. You may think that there can't be any universal application of this commandment because very few people are murderers. I have a notion that you would suspect very few people in your circle of acquaintances of being murderers. But maybe someone in the same room with you right now—without your knowing it—is a murderer! But don't move. I'm not sure that any of us can escape that charge.

Listen to our Lord as He expounds on the sixth commandment and lifts it to the nth degree:

Ye have heard that it was said by them of old, Thou shalt not kill and whosoever shall kill shall be in

danger of judgment; but I say unto you that whosoever is angry with his brother without a cause shall be in danger of judgment; and whosoever shall say to his brother, Raca, shall be in danger of the council; but whosoever shall say, Thou fool, shall be in danger of hell fire. (Matthew 5:21, 22)

Now I think this can be simplified, because there needs to be a transposition here. The second statement concerning *raca* goes with the first. Let me give it like that and see if it doesn't make more sense to you: "You have heard that it was said of old, you shall not kill. Whoever shall kill shall be in danger of the judgment; whoever shall say to his brother, 'Raca,' shall be in danger of the council." The word *raca* means "empty" or "good-for-nothing." The rabbis in Jesus' day said that you could be brought into court and tried for calling someone that.

The Lord Jesus has something else to say about it: "But I say unto you that whoever is angry with his brother without a cause shall be in danger of judgment. Whoever shall say, Thou fool [a fool is a rebel and implies godlessness], shall be in danger of hell fire." That, beloved, is very solemn and serious. When you are driving down the highway, do you ever have someone cut in on you, and you say, "You fool!"? Have you ever done that? If you have, in God's sight you are guilty of murder. Anger is the basis of all murder. Have you ever been so angry with someone that you'd like to choke him? Well, why didn't you go through with it? You were afraid, of course. Also you have a certain background that restrains you. But anger is the thing that's back of murder, and in God's sight anger is murder.

You may be objecting, "I know lovely people, cultured and refined, surely you don't think they're guilty of mur-

der in God's sight!'' Well, they are not if they've never
been angry. If they have been angry, they are murderers
in God's sight. You have heard of sweet, refined women
putting arsenic in tea! In England a very lovely doctor
was killing off his rich patients. And in America a Sunday school superintendent was arrested for murder. It's
in our hearts, friends.

> **For from within, out of the heart of men, proceed
> evil thoughts, adulteries, fornications, murders.**
> (Mark 7:21)

Out of the heart, the Lord Jesus said, proceed about
the ugliest things you have ever seen, and among them
is murder!

Are you prepared to defend yourself before God and
say you have never been angry and that you are not guilty
of murder before Him? Maybe you want to raise some
technical point, as some folk will, that since this commandment is in the Sermon on the Mount, it is not for
us today. Let's turn to one of the last books in the Bible
to be written, the First Epistle of John:

> **Whosoever hateth his brother is a murderer; and ye
> know that no murderer hath eternal life abiding in
> him.** (1 John 3:15)

The Holy Spirit, as God's attorney (for He's called that),
brings a charge against you and against me that we're
murderers in God's sight. May I suggest to you that you
will have a difficult time proving yourself innocent before God. I suggest you plead guilty. Cast yourself upon
the mercy of the Court.

Actually, He has another charge against you also. You
remember Stephen, when he stood on trial before the

Sanhedrin that day, said, referring to Christ, ". . . of whom ye have been now the betrayers and murderers" (Acts 7:52). And there sat Saul of Tarsus, a member of the Sanhedrin, guilty of the murder of Jesus Christ. And I must confess that I share his guilt. I put Him to death. If it hadn't been for my sin, Jesus never would have gone to the Cross, "For he hath made him who knew no sin, to be sin for us, that we might be made the righteousness of God in him" (2 Corinthians 5:21). Jesus Christ was made sin for us, so you and I put Him to death. Why don't you plead guilty?

But you may protest that Peter wrote, "Let none of you suffer [be judged] as a murderer . . ." (1 Peter 4:15). We've got to defend ourselves against the charge here. Oh, I want to tell you that you can defend yourself. There is a city of refuge to which you can flee and find mercy. That city of refuge is Christ.

It is recorded in 2 Samuel 3 that after King Saul died, Abner, his captain, finally deserted to David. However, David's captain, Joab, suspected Abner of being a spy and, wanting to avenge the death of his brother whom Abner had slain in battle, he contrived to get him out of Hebron because Hebron was a city of refuge. I suppose he said something like this, "Come out here, Abner, I've got something to tell you." Abner made the mistake of his life. He came out of the city of refuge, and when he was on neutral ground Joab killed him.

King David went to the funeral and wept at the grave of Abner. He made it plain that he was not guilty of this crime. Notice 2 Samuel 3:33:

And the king lamented over Abner, and said, Died Abner as a fool dieth?

Abner could have been safe in a city of refuge, but he was foolish enough to be lured out and killed.

Friend, you and I stand as sinners before God. How foolish it is to try somehow to defend ourselves and say we are not guilty when God says we are guilty. Oh, to flee to the city of refuge and cast ourselves upon this Savior! The Scripture suggests that you are a fool if you don't do it. "Died Abner as a fool dieth?" Abner could have been safe. And at this moment you can be safe.

How wise it is to come to the Savior—He is our city of refuge—and find safety and security in Him. He saves sinners, even murderers.

> *How firm a foundation,*
> *   ye saints of the Lord,*
> *Is laid for your faith*
> *   in His excellent Word!*
> *What more can He say*
> *   than to you He hath said,*
> *To you, who for refuge*
> *   to Jesus have fled?*
>
> *Fear not, I am with thee,*
> *   O be not dismayed,*
> *For I am thy God,*
> *   and I'll still give thee aid;*
> *I'll strengthen thee, help thee,*
> *   and cause thee to stand,*
> *Upheld by My gracious,*
> *   omnipotent hand.*
> *   —George Keith*

CHAPTER 7

LOVE IS SACRED
The Seventh Commandment

Thou shalt not commit adultery. (Exodus 20:14)

The moral barometer of America has sunk to a new low. Morality is selling below par on the social stock market in this land of ours. There was a time, I remember, when a popular movie star broke the seventh commandment. He was involved in a nasty and ugly scandal, and public opinion condemned him. He was ostracized and relegated to oblivion. If I mentioned his name you probably would not have heard of him. But the tables have turned.

We have seen a breakdown of morals that has turned our nation into a bunch of pagan animals. Our cities and towns have become so lawless that homes are broken into and stores plundered at will. It is dangerous to walk the streets at night; in many places it is dangerous in the daytime. The police seem helpless to handle the situation. Gross immorality prevails. We are overwhelmed by sex. It is taught in our schools, in literature, and on movie and TV screens continually. Marriage is discounted, ignored, or ridiculed.

The basic values of life and home are forsaken. In their place we have crime, dishonesty, lying, abnormal sex, child molestation, drugs, divorce, and homosexuality. The spotlight is on strange and weird conduct and characters. And in this day anyone who says anything against adultery is called prudish and puritanic.

But, my friend, this is merely one of the many symptoms that indicates our contemporary society is morally sick. There was a day when a high moral standard was the unwritten law of the land. Every man and woman had to be married to live together. They established a republic which was stable and produced a law-abiding society where people were free to walk the streets at night and to work in freedom.

After World War I there was a loosening of this moral code. After World War II it was broken, violated and rejected. Pandora's box has been opened, and here are some of the contents: murder, stealing, abortion, drugs, alcohol, deterioration of public education, pornography, homosexuality, poverty, failure of money institutions, communism, psycho-religion, eroding religious freedom, war, terrorism, and political corruption.

Shakespeare has Macbeth say of human life down here, "... A tale told by an idiot, full of sound and fury, signifying nothing." One waggish cafe society commentator has made this statement about divorce. He says, "Judging by the divorce rate, a lot of people who say, 'I do,' don't." May I say to you that we're living in that kind of an hour when contemporary music is the funeral dirge of a fading, wonderful civilization that we have enjoyed.

Even many Christian people today are looking charitably upon the breaking of the seventh commandment. We need to keep in mind that the seventh commandment encompasses all forms of sexual sin. And God spells them out for us in Exodus 22, Leviticus 18 and 20, and Deuteronomy 22. And all too many folk are guilty of these.

Now I'd like to ask the question: Is God today coasting along with the public opinion of the hour? Is God floating down the stream with the majority? Is God altering His program? Has God changed and trimmed His sails and watered down His standards?

Well, may I say to you, my friend, there still stands in the chiseled stone of the centuries the inflexible seventh commandment: "Thou shalt not commit adultery." There's been no new edition of it gotten out from heaven, and God has put out no new version concerning it. It still stands: "Thou shalt not commit adultery." That is still heaven's attitude toward this awful sin of the hour in which we live.

I'd like to gather together four different approaches to this subject: The Home—the foundation of the seventh commandment; Humanity here and now—the application of the seventh commandment; Hell—the violation of the seventh commandment; Heaven—the culmination of the seventh commandment.

The Home—The Foundation of the Seventh Commandment

First of all, I want you to consider with me the home in America, which is the foundation of the seventh commandment. I know it's a trite bromide and a hackneyed chestnut for me to say that the home is the foundation of society. Politicians and preachers have waxed eloquent on that statement through the years. It may have been overworked. But you may be sure of one thing: It is still true today that the home is the foundation of society. And the backbone of the home is marriage, and marriage is the oldest institution in this world.

But, friends, marriage today is certainly being questioned and in some circles repudiated. Therefore, at this time it would be well to go back and look at God's original arrangement in this matter that concerns the seventh commandment.

We find in the Book of Genesis:

Therefore shall a man leave his father and his mother, and shall cleave unto his wife; and they shall be one flesh. (Genesis 2:24)

Marriage is not only the oldest institution, it is a *divine* institution. And the fact of the matter is, it is the *only* institution that man brought with him out of the Garden of Eden. It's the only token we have of the life that was lived yonder in the Garden in the original creation. We are told in this passage that marriage is the highest human relationship. It takes precedence over that which we consider to be the highest, the relationship of parent and child. God says here that a man shall leave his father and his mother. He's brought up in a home under certain circumstances and environments and drawn to father and mother. But there comes a day when he or she establishes another relationship. The one which had been so firm in those early years is now broken, and the new relationship of marriage is established. It is the *highest* human relationship known to man.

The marriage of a Christian man and a Christian woman is a love relationship, and it's not one talking down to the other at all. It is compared to the relationship of Christ and the church: "For the husband is the head of the wife, even as Christ is the head of the church; and he is the savior of the body" (Ephesians 5:23). Now the analogy of the body, you see, is in regard to Christ and the church. Christian marriage down here, if it's made unto the Lord, made by Spirit-filled Christians—for that's to whom Paul is speaking here—it is a miniature of the relationship of Christ and the church, and there is no relationship that can be any sweeter than that.

Will you listen to me very carefully on this. The physical act of marriage is sacred, it's a religious ritual, it's a sacrament. I do not mean a sacrament made by a church nor a man-made ceremony, but it is a sacrament that is made by God Himself, one which He sanctifies. And He says that this relationship is to reveal to you the love of Christ for your soul. Therefore, a man and a woman are to find in each other persons of high moral character to whom they can give themselves wholly and completely, finding perfect fulfillment and satisfaction. It's not the sex appeal that makes marriage—it's the character of the individuals. It's when a man and a woman find in each other that which is worthwhile. That's what makes a marriage, my friend.

We are told that at the creation of the first husband and wife the two were to be made one. God never said they would be *the Adamses*—He said they would be *Adam* (see Genesis 5:2). The two would be one, made one by God's act of marriage. And, my friend, God has not changed His plan concerning it. Therefore God gave the seventh commandment as a shield to protect the home. It was to be a wall of fire separating them from the filth that was on the outside. It was to be a wedding ring of purity surrounding the two that were in it. It was to be a protection surrounding the love of a man for a woman and the love of a woman for a man. As God gave the sixth commandment to protect life—"Thou shalt do no murder"—He likewise gave the seventh commandment to protect the love of man and woman. Therefore, back yonder in the home which God established, He first of all erected the commandment, "The shalt not commit adultery," as a hedge to be put around the home in a world that would be hostile toward it, that would oppose it.

Humanity Here and Now—The Application of the Seventh Commandment

Then, my beloved, that brings me to our second division, dealing with humanity in the day in which we live, and the application of the seventh commandment. Not only of this commandment, but you can say of all the commandments, that they are not rules to obey as a personal favor to God. God never gave the commandments to set up some sort of high hurdle to hinder man in his life and his expression down here. But these commandments were given for the protection and the good of mankind. Even the apostle John, in his first epistle, his letter of love, has written, "His commandments are not burdensome." They were not given to hurt or harm. Therefore, breaking the seventh commandment is one of the most flagrant, atrocious and outrageous crimes in all of God's universe. Actually, there's nothing that will quite compare to it. First of all—let me say this emphatically— it's a sin against the individual and is so stated in God's Word. Over in the Book of Job, I read language like this,

For this is an heinous crime; yea, it is an iniquity to be punished by the judges. For it is a fire that consumeth to destruction . . . (Job 31:11, 12)

That's God estimate of it. And we find, in Proverbs 6:32,

But whoso committeth adultery with a woman lacketh understanding: he that doeth it destroyeth his own soul.

And may I say to you that the breaking of this commandment exacts its penalty upon the complex nature of mankind, both physical and psychological. Today any medical doctor can tell you the effect that adultery has on those involved in it.

My friend, to commit adultery is not only a sin against one's own self, it is also a sin against the family. Think of the multitudes of children who are denied the love and the care and the companionship of one or both of their parents because of the breaking of this commandment! And in many cases the children as well as the adults are physically and emotionally scarred for life. Then think what it's doing to the moral structure of our entire society today.

Against Society

This brings me to say that adultery is also a sin against society. It's like a mine field which has already destroyed many who have entered it. It is the catastrophic and cataclysmic destruction of the morality which had made this country great. None of us seems to grasp the great damage it has done to the individual, the home, the family, the city, the state laws, and to our nation. We are turning out a generation of savages, wimps, and oddballs. Our prisons cannot contain all the criminals. We have totally rejected Bible morality. One television actress said that she had broken four of the Ten Commandments and she intended to break all of them, including murder.

All of a sudden the fabric of our society has changed. Things that were black are now white, and things that were white are now black. And we have great confusion today. We need to keep in mind the the word *adultery* encompases all forms of sexual sins, and God spells it out for us in Exodus, Leviticus and Deuteronomy. And a society is doomed when it redefines what God calls "sin" as an alternate lifestyle. May I say to you, a breakup of the family due to sex outside of marriage is a sin against society.

And somebody needs to speak out on premarital sex. I have a letter from a girl who wants to know if it is all right. She writes: "My fiance says that we should start sleeping together before we get married so we will have an established relationship when we get married. He says it isn't wrong because we're engaged. What does the Bible say?"

Essentially my answer to her was this: "I'll answer the last part of your question first so we will have God's answer. In the Ten Commandments given by God to His people is this: 'Thou shalt not commit adultery.' Since your marriage has not taken place, having sex together is adultery. The request your fiance has made of you raises two questions about him. First, does he really love you or is he confusing love with lust? Second, is he being honest in promising that he will marry you?"

In spite of all this new emphasis on sex before marriage, the divorce courts continue to grind out their monotonous story of the tragedy of modern marriage in ever-increasing numbers. I think it is time that God is heard.

Another vicious attack being made against our sanctity of love and marriage is homosexuality. The important thing for me is, what is the Scripture's position relative to this sort of thing? The Word of God is very clear. There's no misunderstanding. Chapter 19 of the Book of Genesis tells about the destruction of Sodom and Gomorrah, and God destroyed these two cities because they had reached the very lowest level of moral degradation, which is homosexuality. God destroyed these cities and He makes no apology for it.

In the New Testament, it says that although God had been gracious with the Gentiles and kind to them, when they reached a certain level of gross immorality, He gave them up. Three times in a single chapter we're told that God gave them up. That means they had reached the place of no return.

Wherefore, God also gave them up to uncleanness through the lusts of their own hearts, to dishonor their own bodies between themselves, who ex-

**changed the truth of God for a lie, and worshiped
and served the creature more than the Creator, who
is blessed forever. Amen. For this cause God gave
them up unto vile affections; for even their women
did exchange the natural use for that which is
against nature; and likewise also the men, leaving
the natural use of the woman, burned in their lust
one toward another; men with men working that
which is unseemly [shameful], and receiving in
themselves that recompense [penalty] of their error
which was fitting [due].** (Romans 1:24–27)

Now that's what God says. It is His viewpoint. Yet today our society is accepting homosexuality as an alternate lifestyle! And of all things, some churches are
condoning it, which causes some young people to get
involved. One young man wrote me about it. He told how
he was led into homosexuality because he thought it was
all right. When he found out that it was a sin in God's
sight and that he needed to be forgiven, he turned to
Christ and has been delivered from it. Now he attempts
to work with others who have been trapped.

Against the Nation

Homosexuality and all that adultery encompasses is a
sin against the *nation*. In saying these things I recognize
that I'm going against the current. I'm not exactly alone,
but I sure feel lonely in this position today, because the
whole stream is moving in that direction. It is an evidence that we are now reaching the lowest level of moral
degradation in this country. I don't know how much farther we're going to go, but the day will come when God
gives us up, and we'll go down the tube just like all those
great nations of the past. As this moral decline contin-

ues, God is either going to have to judge America or else He will have to apologize to Sodom and Gomorrah for what He did to those two cities because of this very thing. This is a lot more serious than some seem to think that it is. You see, drunkenness and gross immorality are what took Babylon down; they took Greece and Egypt down; they took Rome down. You read their stories. And our young nation is following blindly in their footsteps.

The historian, Gibbon, in his *Decline and Fall of the Roman Empire*, lists five reasons why the great nation of Rome went down, and he includes the break-up of the home as being one of the reasons.

Read *The Iliad*. It tells of the ruin of an adulterer, Paris, and his nation because he took Helen of Troy, who was another man's wife, and ran away with her. When Paris did that, Agamemnon with all of the hosts of the Greeks, set upon his life, and that army stayed there till they wrought vengeance.

And in more recent times there have been men in England, even those who were statesmen, who have said that adultery is treason and that the adulterer should be tried as a traitor to his nation.

Against the Race

Adultery is not only a sin against the nation, it's a sin against the race of mankind, because each of us has a part in either developing or destroying the race of which we are a part. But thank God there is a moral remnant in the human family today, and in spite of the onslaught against it, it is moving forward, and you can hear it marching to the steps of this commandment: "Thou shalt not commit adultery." May I say, I consider myself to be one of that remnant. I shall never forget the night that I met my wife. It was a summer night in Texas, and we were invited to the home of mutual friends for dinner. Frankly, these friends were trying to bring us together. I didn't want to go because I had an engagement in Fort Worth that night. My wife didn't want to go because she was going with another fellow! But that night when I saw her—I never shall forget her dark hair, her brown eyes—there in the candlelight I looked at her, and I fell in love with her. I proposed to her on our second date, and the reason I didn't propose on that first date was that I didn't want her to think I was in a hurry! She had never won a beauty contest, but she was beautiful. How wonderful it was!

I believe in love at first sight, I believe in it very strongly. Although I proposed to my wife on the second date we had, don't get any wrong ideas. It was a year before we got married. We wanted to make sure. Yes, I believe in love at first sight, but I think love ought to be tested by quite a bit of time before marriage takes place.

Now love ought to be in your heart and life if you are a believer. But, friend, if there are sensual sins in your life, you will never know what real love is. There are many young people today who know a great deal about sex, but they know nothing about love. Love is a fruit of the Spirit, and God will give this love to a husband for his wife and to a wife for her husband. I don't think anyone can love like two Christians can love. My, how they can love each other!

The night I first proposed to Ruth she did not accept me, but when she did, we had prayer and dedicated our lives to the Lord. I told her, "I am a preacher who speaks out plainly. I may get into trouble someday. We may find ourselves out on the street." I shall never forget what she said to me: "Well, I'll just beat the drum for you if you have to get out on the street!" That is love on a higher plane.

When we lost our first little girl, I did not want the doctor to tell my wife—I wanted to tell her myself. When I gave her the news, we wept together and then we prayed. Love like that is the fruit of the Holy Spirit.

> **And I will betroth thee unto me ... in righteousness, and in justice, and in lovingkindness, and in mercies. I will even betroth thee unto me in faithfulness; and thou shalt know the Lord.** (Hosea 2:19, 20)

We are seeing something very wonderful here. God is speaking to the nation Israel. The word *betroth* means literally to woo a virgin; it means to court a girl. If you are a married man, you can remember when your wife was a girl and how pretty she was and how you courted her. You said a lot of sweet things then.

The other evening my wife and I were sitting out on the patio. I was recuperating from surgery, and we were just talking about the fact that we are getting old. I took a look at her, and I would have to say that she is getting old like I am. But I can remember that girl I first saw down in Texas with her hair as black as a raven's wing and those flashing brown eyes. She had a sultry look, let me tell you, because her complexion is dark.

As we remembered those wonderful days, we got just a little sentimental. We talked about the times when we used to drive up to Fort Worth to eat in a restaurant there. We ordered steaks, and do you know what we paid for a steak in that day? It was fifty cents apiece! She was a schoolteacher, and I was a poor preacher so I made her pay for her own—even at fifty cents! I've tried to make up for that through the years since then, I can assure you.

To woo a virgin is a wonderful experience. That is what God said He would do to Israel. What a beautiful, lovely picture this is. God says, "I intend to win you for Myself." But man has spoiled what God ordained as the most wonderful experience in life.

Against God

Then finally, my beloved, adultery is a sin against God. There was a man, one of the great men of Scripture, of whom it was said he was "a man after God's own heart" (Acts 13:22). Yet this man committed the sin of adultery!

Apparently David had stayed home from the war in which his nation was engaged. He should have been with his men on the field. I have a notion it was the first time David had ever stayed home during wartime. Well, he looked. His look led to the act. Because he was king, he could have his way. He thought that, since he was the king and known as a man of God, he might get by with it. But, oh, my friend, nobody gets by with adultery. He attempted to cover it up.

So there came a day when God sent the prophet Nathan to him with a story of injustice in his kingdom. David, that redheaded king, could rise in anger when the wrong was somewhere else. And he said, ". . . As the LORD liveth, the man who hath done this thing shall surely die" (2 Samuel 12:5). I submit the prophet Nathan as the bravest man you'll ever find. Nathan pointed the finger at David the king and said, "Thou art the man!" Then David went yonder into the presence of God—and listen to his confession,

Have mercy upon me, O God, according to thy loving-kindness; according unto the multitude of thy tender mercies blot out my transgressions. Wash me thoroughly from mine iniquity, and cleanse me from

my sin. For I acknowledge my transgressions, and my sin is ever before me. Against thee, thee only, have I sinned, and done this evil in thy sight, that thou mightest be justified when thou speakest, and be clear when thou judgest. Behold, I was shaped in iniquity, and in sin did my mother conceive me. (Psalm 51:1–5)

And if you want to see the psychological effect of that sin upon a man, you read the confession of David in Psalm 32:3, 4;

When I kept silence, my bones became old through my roaring all the day long. For day and night thy hand was heavy upon me; my moisture is turned into the drought of summer. Selah.

If you want to know whether sin hurts or not, read the story of that man who lost his joy, the joy of his salvation and with it everything worthwhile:

Restore unto me the joy of thy salvation, and uphold me with a willing spirit. Then will I teach transgressors thy ways, and sinners shall be converted unto thee. (Psalm 51:12,13)

He knew he was dirty and cried out to God for cleansing. That's not all. He said something else that is very significant: "Against thee, thee only, have I sinned, and done this evil in thy sight . . ." (Psalm 51:4). Adultery is a sin against Almighty God.

What Does God Mean by Adultery?

Well, let's look back at the sixth commandment where God says literally, "Thou shalt do no murder" (Exodus

20:13). And then a little later God put down degrees—
first degree murder, second degree murder, manslaughter, accidental killing, and many others. But may I say
this to you: In the seventh commandment, there is no
degree of adultery at all. Adultery is adultery, and it
never changes, it never becomes anything else. Note this
statement of the Lord Jesus in Matthew 5:32:

**But I say unto you that whosoever shall put away
[divorce] his wife, except for the cause of fornication, causeth her to commit adultery; and whosoever
shall marry her that is divorced committeth adultery.**

Now notice that right there our Lord combined what
men today are trying to separate by saying that there are
degrees in adultery. There's no such thing as degrees in
adultery at all. If sex is committed by a person who is
single, it is sin against the marriage of the future. If the
person is married, adultery is a sin against the marriage
that is.

In Matthew 5 we see the Lord Jesus Christ take the
sixth commandment and lift it to the nth degree. Did you
know that He did likewise with the seventh commandment? I've often thought that He probably did it with all
ten of the commandments, which puts them in the realm
where any person in our day must cry out to God for
mercy. But will you note as our Lord lifts this seventh
commandment to the nth degree:

**Ye have heard that it was said by them of old, Thou
shalt not commit adultery; but I say unto you that
whosoever looketh on a woman to lust after her hath
committed adultery with her already in his heart.**
(Matthew 5:27, 28)

He says here that the desire itself is sinful. It is the "look" that leads to the act. We fall into sin by entertaining the thought that leads to it. It was Augustine, speaking of this sin, who said, "An evil thought passes thy door first as a stranger, then it enters as a guest, then it installs itself as a master." That's the way sin gets into our lives, friend. And it was Martin Luther who said that you can't keep the birds from flying over your head, but you can keep them from building a nest in your hair. And that's exactly, I think, what our Lord meant about this sin of adultery.

For instance, we read today of a brutal murder, or we see a senseless crime, and it's repulsive. We abhor it. There's no temptation to have any part in that. But, my beloved, adultery is different. You let the mind dwell on it, and you are tempted to do it. It's one of the sins of the imagination.

Sex is one of the drives of mankind. And it is said that sex and hunger are the strongest appetites of man. That's my reason for saying there is too much information and instruction about sex being given to young people in school and church. The subject of sex is dynamite. The quietness of people when I speak on it is an evidence of that. May I say to you that it should not be dwelt on as much as it is today. And with teenagers and younger children there is entirely too great an emphasis put on the boy/girl relationship. But sexuality outside of marriage is something that our Lord reached out and put His finger on, lifting the commandment, "Thou shalt not commit adultery," to the nth degree so that every man must wilt before it.

I remember in my first pastorate a man who came down to speak to me one morning—a big, red-faced fellow—and he said to me, "You made the statement this morning, young man, that nobody keeps the Ten Com-

mandments or *can* keep the Ten Commandments. I want
you to know that you're looking at a man right now who
keeps the Ten Commandments." I said to him, "I'm willing to take your word for it after I examine you. Will you
let me examine you?" He said, "Go ahead." I said to him,
"The Ten Commandments say, 'Thou shalt not commit
adultery.' Our Lord lifted that commandment to the nth
degree by saying that if you so much as look upon a
woman to lust for her you're guilty of adultery. Do you
want to look me straight in the eye and say to me this
morning that you're not guilty?" That man ducked his
head, grunted some kind of epithet, turned on his heels
and walked out. And up to the present day, he hasn't
answered me. I say to you that here is a command that
will blanch your soul if you attempt to say before Almighty God, "I stand on this ground and I'm not guilty
at all."

Hell—The Violation of the
Seventh Commandment

The Mosaic Law exacted the death penalty for breaking
this law. I'm not going to turn to all the passages dealing
with it in the Mosaic system, but I will give you the one
found in Leviticus 20:10:

**And the man who committeth adultery with another
man's wife, even he who committeth adultery with
his neighbor's wife, the adulterer and the adulteress
shall surely be put to death.**

My friend, that law was enforced in Israel, and the person who was guilty of breaking it was stoned to death.

That changes the complexion of what the apostle Paul said in Romans 7:2, which I often hear quoted.

"For the woman who hath an husband is bound by the law to her husband as long as he liveth; but if the husband be dead, she is loosed from the law of her husband.

Some folk insist that divorce and remarriage is not permitted under any circumstances according to this verse. We need to thoroughly understand the background. What would happen under the Mosaic Law if a man or woman were unfaithful in marriage? Suppose a woman is married to a man who is a philanderer, and he is unfaithful to her. What happens? He is stoned to death. When the old boy is lying under a pile of stones, she is free to marry another, of course. In our day we cannot apply the Mosaic Law—we can't stone to death the unfaithful. If this law were being enforced and the guilty persons were stoned to death, it would be very difficult to walk through Southern California. We would have to go around too many rock piles! Also it would mean that a great many people would have been stoned to death who are still alive today. But in God's sight when either husband or wife breaks the seventh commandment, that one is *dead* to the innocent spouse.

Oh, my friend, God exacted the death penalty for those who broke this commandment, and there was no mercy. And I'm of the opinion that He has not changed that part of it. You will notice this when you come to the Epistle to the Hebrews,

Marriage is honorable in all, and the bed undefiled, but fornicators and adulterers God will judge. (Hebrews 13:4)

And if you turn to the last two chapters of the Bible where God gives the wonderful picture of heaven, you will find the Spirit of God felt it necessary to say that on the *outside* are the sexually immoral and they shall not enter that heavenly city.

And there shall in no way enter into it anything that defileth, neither he that worketh abomination, or maketh a lie, but they who are written in the Lamb's book of life. (Revelation 21:27)

But outside are dogs and sorcerers and sexually immoral and murderers and idolaters, and whoever loves and practices a lie. (Revelation 22:15 NKJV)

That is God's law, and that is God's Word. Someone says to me, "Preacher, that is indeed a severe penalty!" I agree with you.

Heaven—The Culmination of the Seventh Commandment

Then, finally, will you look with me at heaven, the culmination of the seventh commandment. Thinking back to the two tablets of stone of Exodus 32:15, 16, there is a relationship between the second commandment and the seventh commandment. The second commandment is "Thou shalt not make unto thee any carved image, or any likeness of anything that is in heaven above, or that is in the earth beneath . . . ." The seventh commandment, which seems to be its parallel, is "Thou shalt not commit adultery."

Idolatry in Israel was called spiritual adultery. It is the sin that God depicts as the most loathsome in the world. And the worst chapter in the Bible, as far as I can tell, is Revelation 17. It's the most frightful scene you can find anywhere. There you see a church—a false church, an apostate church—which has turned from God and is depicted as a harlot, riding the Beast. Oh, my friend, God judged His nation Israel for the sin of spiritual adultery. He said through Jeremiah the prophet, before His people were taken into captivity, "Backsliding Israel has committed adultery!" They committed spiritual adultery in that they turned from the living and true God. They had gone after the idols of the heathen. They had turned from Him.

Likewise today the relationship between Christ and the believer is spoken of as that between bridegroom and bride. When someday the church is presented to Him without spot and without blemish, it will be a relationship that's the very highest. When Jesus' mother and His brethren came to Him, you will recall that He sent back a word which sounded almost cruel, "Who is My mother, and who are My brothers?" And then He said, "Anyone who will do the will of My Father which is in heaven is My mother and My brother and My sister." In other words, in Matthew 12:46-50 He established a new relationship which is higher than that between a man and his own unsaved children. This is the relationship between God and a lost sinner who is found. Paul wrote this, and I think he's speaking about both here:

Know ye not that the unrighteous shall not inherit the kingdom of God? Be not deceived: neither fornicators [having premarital sex], nor idolaters, nor adulterers, nor effeminate, nor abusers of themselves with mankind . . . shall inherit the kingdom of God. (1 Corinthians 6:9,10)

Now I'm sure that there is someone thinking, "Well, if that's true, there's not much hope for me. In fact, there is no hope for me at all." My friend, there is an incident in Scripture which reveals that there is hope for any person. You will find it in John 8:1-11. (Although some Bibles omit it, I believe it belongs in the Word of God.) It is the episode of a woman said to be guilty of adultery and taken in the very act—how harsh and how crude those men were who brought her into the temple area, right into the presence of the Lord Jesus, and into the middle of the group as He was teaching! And every man who came had a rock in his hand, was ready to stone her, and they said to Him, "Our law says she is to be stoned. What do You say?" Without even looking up, Jesus began writing on the sand there in the temple area. Then He said, "The one who is without sin among you, let him throw the first stone." Well, there were not any stones thrown that day. And we're told that beginning with the oldest down to the youngest they put down their rocks and slipped out as quietly as they could. Finally, that woman was left with the only Man who could have stoned her, and He said to her, "Neither do I condemn you. Go, and sin no more."

This frightful thing of sexual sins, this awful thing which is a sin against humanity and a sin against God, can be forgiven, for there is a Savior who died on the cross for those who are guilty and will trust Him.

But God commendeth his love toward us in that, while we were yet sinners, Christ died for us. (Romans 5:8)

For he hath made him [Jesus Christ**], who knew no sin to be sin for us, that we might be made the righteousness of God in him.** (2 Corinthians 5:21)

Oh, my friend, I want you to see the heart of God as He restated these Ten Commandments to a new generation. The generation that had originally heard the Law at Mount Sinai was dead. Their bones were bleaching out there in the desert. This new generation, the Israel that was actually going into the Promised Land—and you and I—will hear it from Moses after forty years of experience with it in the wilderness.

Listen to God's heart-cry for His people:

Oh, that there were such an heart in them, that they would fear me, and keep all my commandments always, that it might be well with them and with their children forever! (Deuteronomy 5:29)

CHAPTER 8

STOP, THIEF!
The Eighth Commandment

Thou shalt not steal. (Exodus 20:15)

W e have now come to the eighth commandment, which is "Thou shalt not steal." We have come also to another invisible division in the Ten Commandments. The first four commandments have to do with a man's relationship to God. The last six have to do with a man's relationship to man. The invisible division has to do with the penalty for breaking the commandment.

The penalty for breaking the first seven commandments was the death penalty. But beginning with the eighth commandment, the offences do not seem to be as severe, for we find that the death penalty is not invoked. In Exodus 22:1 we read,

If a man shall steal an ox, or a sheep, and kill it, or sell it, he shall restore five oxen for an ox, and four sheep for a sheep.

However, there were exceptions even to this law, and you find in the very next verse that "if a thief be found breaking in and be smitten that he die, there shall no blood be shed for him." In other words, if a thief is caught in the act of stealing, and if that thief dies as a result, a murder charge would not be leveled against the person who had killed him.

There is one other exception that is given to us. In Exodus 21:16 we read:

**And he that stealeth a man, and selleth him, or if he
be found in his hand, he shall surely be put to death.**

In other words, the selling of a person into slavery was
punishable by death.

Now the commandment "Thou shalt not steal" is probably broken more than any of the other commandments.
And this is certainly true in our contemporary culture.
Stealing has become so commonplace that we speak today of the "common thief."

It may surprise you to learn that although thievery is
rampant in our day, we have to read over halfway through
the Bible chronologically before we find any record of
stealing or before any thief is identified. For instance, up
to the time of the Flood when God destroyed practically
the entire race, it was not for any act of stealing, as far as
we know. There was not one thief in the crowd, at least
they were not identified as such. Probably there was stealing, but it was not the prevailing sin of that day.

When we come to the Tower of Babel, there was no thief
whom God arrested there. Thievery was not the reason He
scattered mankind at the Tower of Babel. When we come
to the destruction of Sodom and Gomorrah, may I say,
stealing was not one of the reasons that God destroyed
that city. And when we come to that long record of Abraham and of Isaac and we see that their faults are recorded
as well as their good points, we do not find that they were
guilty at any time of this act of stealing.

It's not until we come to Jacob that we find stealing
mentioned. And the very interesting thing is that stealing
is not mentioned in connection with Jacob at all! It is
mentioned with his lovely Rachel, for she stole the images,
the gods of her father Laban, and that was the excuse
Laban gave for following them as they headed back to the
land of Israel.

Jacob, though, was a thief and is so labeled elsewhere because he stole the birthright from his brother. From then on we find stealing becoming one of the great sins of the human family, and God added the eighth commandment chiseled in stone to block man in his sinful career.

Achan, for instance, the man who caused Israel's humiliating defeat at the little town of Ai and almost caused the entire nation to forfeit the Promised Land, was ferreted out, and his sin is identified as stealing. It was a sin so serious to God that it could have kept these people out of the land.

And when that man confessed his sin, we find laid before us the entire psychology of stealing today. Here is what Achan said:

> **When I saw among the spoils a beautiful Babylonish garment, and two hundred shekels of silver, and a wedge of gold of fifty shekels weight, *then* I coveted them, and took them. . . .** (Joshua 7:21)

That's the threefold process of every thief. He sees something he wants, then he covets it, and then he takes it—he commits the act. That is the psychology of every thief from the day of Achan down to the present hour.

And you will find in the nation Israel that the thief was despised above all others who committed sin. In Proverbs 6:30 it is put in rather a positive note: "Men do not despise a thief, if he steal to satisfy his soul when he is hungry." And the thought, of course, is that they *do* despise the thief if he steals on any other basis.

And the greatest villain in the Scriptures, Judas Iscariot who betrayed our Lord, is identified in the Word of God as being a thief. He had the bag; that is, he was the treasurer of the group, and he carried what was put in it. That's the one thing that identifies this man and causes him to stand out.

Now I'd like for us to establish who a thief is and just what is stealing. And I do not want to adopt our modern, legal language because it becomes greatly involved today. Nor do I want to get the opinion of the man on the street because he has been wrong about too many things. And, of course, somebody suggests, "Then let's go to Webster's Dictionary." Well, Webster will not be helpful to us because here is one place where Webster had his tongue in his cheek. This is the way he defines a thief: "A thief is one who steals." And when you look up the word *steal*, it means to practice theft! That, to my judgment, is beating around the bush, my beloved. Stealing makes a thief and a thief steals—we're not helped very much by those definitions.

May I give you a very practical, and I believe a biblical, definition of what it means to steal: To steal is to take anything that rightly belongs to someone else, to take it either secretly or by force. Or we might put it in the common colloquialism of the hour, which is the philosophy that says, "Let's get something for nothing." My friend, this is the great sin of America today.

A cynic has remarked, "This is the land of the free and the home of the knave." And another cynic has said that this age in which we live will go down in history as the Age of Chiselry. Our crime bill today is astronomical. Our jails are so overcrowded that criminals are released for lack of space to house them. The problem is so widespread that employers in the United States are losing hundreds of millions of dollars each year through their employees' dishonesty.

Several years ago a couple of writers made a trip across America with an old broken-down car, a regular beat-up jalopy, and that meant they had to stop in many garages. Now this is not my estimate, this is what they said: "Three out of five garagemen will overcharge, lie, invent unnecessary work or charge for work not done, for new parts and parts not installed." May I say to you that we could multiply these figures and show that America is certainly letting this particular commandment, "Thou shalt not steal," be broken more than any other one of the commandments. It's the favorite commandment to break in America today.

Now I know that there are some folk who are saying, "This is one commandment, Preacher, you can't pin on us. Perhaps we did harbor hatred in our hearts which makes us guilty of breaking the sixth commandment, 'Thou shalt not kill.' Perhaps we have entertained impure thoughts and are guilty of breaking the seventh commandment, 'Thou shalt not commit adultery,' but you dare not suggest that we're guilty of this contemptible and despicable sin of stealing. Surely you do not think that any of us would stoop so low today as to steal?"

Well, may I say to you, I do not believe that there's anyone of us who could be called a common crook or a pickpocket or a shoplifter or a kleptomaniac or a stickup man or a bank robber or an embezzler or a racketeer or a gangster. And I have a notion that there's not one of us who is in partnership with a drug cartel or in any illegal business enterprise.

My beloved, I do not make that sort of charge. I do not believe that anyone of us would put a gun in the ribs of another individual in a dark alley in order to take from him something that he possesses.

Gambling Is Stealing

It is not my intention to talk about the obvious and the common types of stealing. Nor am I going to deal

with the complicated cleverness of crooks in this intricate business world of modern life today. And I'm not
going to talk about forms of socialism and communism
which are types of stealing, by the way.

But I do want to put the label of stealing on those
types which are overlooked and are generally passed by.
First of all let me say that gambling is stealing. The
gambler is a refined thief, but he acts from the same
motive as does any thief. It's always, for him, something
for nothing. He is the one man who acts on the theory
that you can beat God's law of "whatever a man soweth,
that shall he also reap," (Galatians 6:7). He thinks that
he is the exception to the rule—that he does not have to
sow anything and yet he can have a bountiful harvest.
These smart boys today know how to get grapes off a
thornbush. They know how to gather figs off thistles.
And every gambler is a vain and egotistical individual.
He can live in luxury, he can drive fancy sport cars, he
can wear the latest styles, his palm does not have to be
calloused and he lives by his wits while poor fools such
as you and I have to work for a living. He's much smarter
than we are—so he thinks.

And if you do not believe that this is big business today,
billions are spent annually in America on gambling—
at least that's what has come out in the open. There is
probably an equal amount that no one ever hears about,
for it's the inclination of the American people, and for
that matter all people, to want to take a chance.

P. T. Barnum certainly was right. The only thing is,
Barnum said, "There's a sucker born every minute," and
now there are *two* born every minute. That's the only
difference today, and it is known from the Gallup Poll
that over twenty percent of the population in America
gamble even in churches.

Today the American public is given over to this vice of

gambling, so much so that the lotteries, places like Las Vegas and the racetracks parade as big business and strut without blushing before the public, calling themselves legitimate enterprises.

Quiz shows come under this category. They are one of the most popular forms of television entertainment in America today. They look innocent enough because we see grandmothers on them, and preachers and even children are appearing on them. The church has never yet lifted its voice in opposition, but I remember when social workers all across America began to protest, saying that children are given a false set of values when they're told they can get something for nothing in this life. My friend, the only thing in this life that costs you nothing is salvation, and the Son of God paid a tremendous price so that you and I might have it.

May I say that gambling today is a form of stealing.

Overcharging

Then there is the second type of stealing that I would like to put the label on today, and that is overcharging. In the business world it's considered clever if you take advantage and charge an exorbitant price. May I say to you that the clever businessman who puts over a deal like that is in God's sight a thief. It is the same as stealing. The apostle Paul says to believers that we are to be honest in all matters, "Providing for honest things, not only in the sight of the Lord but also in the sight of men" (2 Corinthians 8:21). And he's not talking there merely about refraining from holding up a bank, he's talking about our business dealings and all of our other dealings, my beloved. A person today who overcharges in the business world is a man or woman who is guilty of breaking the eighth commandment.

Robbing God

And then, my beloved, there is another way that people are guilty of breaking this commandment. God is the One who has labeled them—I did not do it—folk who rob God.

It was in the declining years of the nation Israel, when they had reached a very low ebb, that the people had become cynical and were talking back to God as He made this charge against them. In Malachi 3:8, God asked the question, "Will a man rob God?" You don't believe he will? God says, "Yet ye have robbed me." Of course these people pleaded innocent. God continued, "But ye say, How have we robbed thee?" And God came right through with the charge, "In tithes and offerings."

Oh, how many Christians today are blessed bountifully with the good of this earth! Let me make this personal. God has blessed *you* materially, and you are withholding from God that which ought to go to Him and to His work. God asks, "Will a man rob God?" And the answer coming from heaven is, "A man *will* rob God," and a man does rob God when he withholds from Him his gifts, his tithes and his offerings.

Now let's move into a realm where more people are guilty. It is the realm of that which is intangible because, you know, there are intangible valuables. Valuables that people steal can be both tangible and intangible. There are certain things that you can take away from a person which are neither money nor assets. They don't come under the heading of chattel or real estate at all. Here is one—and please follow me very carefully through these.

According to Scripture, to be reluctant or to refuse to do what we know is right is sin. James, that very practical man, wrote in his epistle:

Therefore, to him that knoweth to do good, and doeth it not, to him it is sin. (James 4:17)

You may remember the story in Luke about a man who went down from Jerusalem to Jericho.

And Jesus, answering, said, A certain man went down from Jerusalem to Jericho, and fell among thieves, who stripped him of his raiment, and wounded him, and departed, leaving him half dead. And by chance there came down a certain priest that way: and when he saw him, he passed by on the other side. And likewise a Levite, when he was at the place, came and looked on him, and passed by on the other side. But a certain Samaritan, as he journeyed, came where he was; and when he saw him, he had compassion on him, and went to him, and bound up his wounds, pouring in oil and wine, and set him on his own beast, and brought him to an inn, and took care of him. (Luke 10:30–34)

It is quite interesting the way the Lord told that parable. He said that the man fell among thieves. And we sometimes think He meant only the gang that beat him up and took all of his possessions. But our Lord said that a priest went by and a Levite went by. The man fell among thieves, all right, but *all* of them were thieves. The thieves who took his money and beat him up and left him half dead were positive and aggressive. The priest and Levite were negative and passive—they just looked at him and passed by on the other side. Let me repeat:

. . . To him that knoweth to do good, and doeth it not, to him it is sin. (James 4:17)

Refusing to do what we know is right is a form of stealing and is so identified in the Word of God.

Someone put it in these lines:

> *I never cut my neighbor's throat*
> *   My neighbor's purse I never stole,*
> *I never spoiled his house and land*
> *   But God have mercy on my soul,*
> *For I am haunted night and day*
> *   By all the deeds I have not done.*
> *O unattempted loveliness,*
> *   O costly valor never won.*

And then, my beloved, there is another very intangible thing that is stolen today. You can rob a man of his reputation. You can steal the most valuable thing that a person has without putting a gun in his ribs or without drawing a knife on him. I mean simply this: When you whisper a lie, when you repeat a bit of gossip, when you start a false rumor against others, you are stealing the most valuable thing they have, their reputation.

Let me illustrate. When I went to the last church I pastored, I was not asked to invest a million dollars there—it would have been foolish of them to have required that, because I did not have a million dollars. But I went, taking the most valuable thing I have, my reputation as a minister.

My beloved, if I had brought a million dollars and you had stolen it, I might recoup it. But when you steal the most valuable thing I have, my reputation, you have stolen that which can never be repaired or returned. It was Shakespeare who has the villain Iago in *Othello* say,

> Who steals my purse steals trash; 'tis
>   something, nothing;
> 'Twas mine, 'tis his, and has been slave to
>   thousands;
> But he that filches from me my good name
> Robs me of that which not enriches him
> And makes me poor indeed.

Oh, my friend, this very day the worst thief there is in your town is not the person who breaks into the back window of your home at night. The worst thief is the person who would steal from you your reputation by whispering a bit of gossip about you. That person is a thief in God's sight. When you steal that which is intangible, you're stealing the most valuable thing in this life.

A Debt to the World

Now, my friend, I am confident that there are many who are saying to me, "Preacher, you haven't even touched me today. I come under none of those categories." Well, I do believe that after I mention the next one, there will not be a person who can stand and say, "I pay my honest debts."

Paul wrote to the Romans when he was ready to go to Rome, "I am debtor both to the Greeks and to the barbarians; both to the wise and to the unwise" (Romans 1:14). And Paul continued, "I am ready to preach the gospel, I am ready to pay this debt."

When Paul the apostle met Jesus Christ on the Damascus Road and came to grips with Him, he who had been under the Law was now brought out and redeemed by grace, which brought him into a right relationship with the living Savior. Paul at that moment discovered that he was a debtor to every man on topside of this earth, both to the Greeks, the civilized, and to the barbarians, the uncivilized; both to the wise, the intellectuals, and the unwise, the ignorant. Paul says it doesn't make any difference who he is, I'm debtor to him, not because I've made a bill with him but because of the fact I've received the gospel of the grace of God and until everyone hears it, I am a debtor.

My friend, at this moment no Christian can stand up, look God in the face and say, "Lord, I've paid my honest debts." Until every last man and woman on topside of this earth hears the gospel, we are debtors, *we* are debtors, we are *debtors*, right now to a lost world outside, and until they hear, we have not paid our honest debts.

Somebody says, "Well, that doesn't let any of us out." No, my friend, it doesn't, including the preacher in the pulpit. And every person today who is a Christian will say to God, "I have not yet paid my debts. I'm a debtor today to an unsaved world."

Why did God let *us* hear the gospel, when this very day there are at least nine hundred million people in our world who have never heard it. I'll never understand why God has been so gracious to us. I'm sure it's not because we're superior in any way. But for some strange reason, He has let you and me have the gospel—that Christ died for our sins, was buried, and rose again (see 1 Corinthians 15:1-4). And I do know this, He says that this privilege has a tremendous responsibility attached to it because the gospel is to be given to every person on topside of the earth!

But don't be discouraged—I have good news today for

the thief. Christ was crucified on a cross, a cross that belonged to another man. The cross had been made for Barabbas and, according to the Gospel of John, Barabbas was a robber. I do not know why, but the Lord Jesus died on a cross where the man's sin was that of robbery. Although His death paid the penalty for every kind of sin, robbery is a specific sin for which He died. He took a robber's place.

And that's not all. He died between two thieves. He was included with the thieves that day when the crucifixion was taking place. Rome usually didn't crucify only a few men at a time. Rome was in the wholesale business, not retail. Rome that day may have crucified nearer to three hundred men than three men, and there was one division where thieves were crucified and Jesus died among thieves. Why? Because He can save thieves. We know that He did save one of them. Someone has said, "He saved one so that no man need despair, but He saved only one that no man dare presume."

> *Three men shared death upon a hill,*
> *But only one man died.*
> *A thief and God Himself made rendezvous.*
> *Three crosses still*
> *Are borne up Calvary's hill*
> *Where sin still lifts them high*
> *Upon the one hang broken men who cursing die;*
> *The other holds the praying thief*
> *And those who, penitent as he,*
> *Still find the Christ beside them on the tree.*
>
> *—Anonymous*

My friend, the thief when saved has to do something that no other sinner has to do. For instance, if a man murders he can be forgiven, but he can't bring the person he killed back to life. The man who commits adultery cannot undo that act. But the man who steals can make restitution. And doing so is the proof of his salvation.

We have an example of this in Luke 19. Our Lord went through Jericho, and He stopped off for dinner at the home of a thief, the biggest rascal in Jericho—and at that time Jericho had some big ones. His name was Zacchaeus, the publican. I don't know what happened inside his home while Jesus was there, but after a little while the Lord and Zacchaeus came outside, and I hear Zacchaeus say, "Behold, Lord, the half of my goods I give to the poor; and if I have taken anything from any man by false accusation, I restore him fourfold." Fourfold was according to the Mosaic Law. He was a thief and he knew he was a thief. He confessed it, and he made restitution. An injunction given to us today is:

Let him that stole steal no more but, rather, let him labor, working with his hands the thing which is good, that he may have to give to him that needeth. (Ephesians 4:28)

That's what Zacchaeus did.

Paul, writing to the Corinthians said, "Providing for honest things . . . in the sight of [all] men" (2 Corinthians 8:21). And again to the Romans he said, "Let us walk honestly, as in the day . . ." (Romans 13:13). Peter says to us, "But let none of you suffer as a murderer, or as a thief, or as an evildoer . . ." (1 Peter 4:15). And then he said to us, positively, "Having your behavior [your manner of life] honest among the Gentiles . . . " (1 Peter 2:12). It was Alexander Pope who wrote, "An honest man is the noblest work of God."

I close with this story. Many years ago in the city of

Chicago there was a very wealthy bachelor, a member of a fashionable church, who heard a great evangelist preach in those days. He came under great conviction of sin, and when he went home he got down on his knees, and he took Christ as his Savior. But he found no peace, no peace of heart whatsoever. Then there came to his remembrance a great sin of the past. He knew that back yonder in his hometown was a girl whom he had betrayed. He had stolen the most priceless thing she had: her virtue. And like the low coward he was, he had run off and left her. He knew he could never have peace until he made some sort of amends or restitution.

And this bachelor, who had become immensely wealthy in Chicago, caught a train and went back to his hometown. When he got there, he made inquiry for the girl and found that she was dead but that the child she had borne, a boy, had been placed in an orphans' home. So he went to the orphans' home and completed all the legal procedure to adopt the boy, his son.

When he took him back to Chicago and brought him into his great home, he knelt right down by the side of the boy and said to him, "Son, could you forgive your father if he had done your mother an awful wrong?" The little fellow looked puzzled and said, "I don't know." This man said, "If you can, son, put your arms around my neck and call me father." After that this wealthy bachelor's testimony was this: "When I accepted Christ as my Savior, there was no peace in my heart. But the day that little fellow put his arms around my neck, the peace of God came into my heart."

He had made restitution.

CHAPTER 9

GOD'S LIE DETECTOR
The Ninth Commandment

Thou shalt not bear false witness against thy neighbor. (Exodus 20:16)

While I was preparing this message on the ninth commandment, a group of us preachers went down to a place in old Chinatown that a missionary who had spent many years in China had discovered. He had arranged for us to be served a very unusual Chinese dinner, one with real Chinese flavoring in some exotic dishes. After the meal, though, we had the usual dessert that you get with this type of restaurant. There were almond cookies and also the fortune cookies with that little piece of paper that some folk like to think predicts their future, but generally it only contains a bit of good advice. With this message about lying in mind, the little piece of paper in my cookie had a very pertinent message for me. It said, "Be cautious in what you say and how you say it!" And I took it as very good advice, because this message comes closer to the man in the pulpit than any other of the Ten Commandments.

I'm speaking first of all to the preachers. It may not have a word for you, but it does have something for the man in the pulpit. I would like to use as a preface the statement of David in Psalm 141:3,

Set a watch, O Lord, before my mouth; keep the door of my lips.

I have spent over 25 hours in preparing this message, and I'm giving it in love. I would rather take any other subject than this, but I believe the man who stands in the pulpit has a responsibility, and I believe that though I may be speaking to myself, it will be applicable to others also.

David, you remember, wrote, "I said in my haste, All men are liars" (Psalm 116:11). Dr. W. I. Carroll, years ago, said to us in class, "I've had a long time to think it over, and I still agree with David." My friend, this is a commandment for us today.

You may feel this commandment is harsh and brutal, that it is like pouring salt in a fresh wound. If I came up to you personally and said, "Thou shalt not bear false witness against thy neighbor," you would say to me, "Dr. McGee, you're impudent—you're positively insulting!" I would indeed be fortunate if I didn't come off with bodily harm!

But suppose someone had circulated a false report concerning you, and it had damaged your reputation. It hurt you terribly and robbed your peace of mind. Then I come to you and say, "I'm sorry that So-and-So has said this concerning you. I regret it a great deal, and they should not have said it. They should know God's commandment that 'thou shalt not bear false witness against thy neighbor.'" These words would then be tender to you. They would be like the balm of Gilead to your hurt soul.

So it is merely our attitude and our relationship toward this commandment that we're looking at.

Simply stated, the ninth commandment, "Thou shalt not bear false witness against thy neighbor," forbids the lie and condemns the liar. This commandment says that any report or word which is designed or destined to hurt another human being comes within the purview of the commandment. It has many ramifications and implications. A bromide of many years says that sin has many tools, but a lie is the handle that fits all of them. Here is that, my beloved, which God is speaking to hearts even in this hour in which we are living.

Now I propose to speak on three aspects of this hydra-headed monster: the origination of the lie; the identification of the lie; the destination of the lie.

Origination of the Lie

Although the lie is complicated and intricate, it is easy to track down its origin. It is easy to locate the culprit. It is easy to find the originator of it, and the reason is that we have God's lie detector. The Word of God is God's lie detector, and it will help us in our understanding.

I want to turn to One whom I consider an authority on this subject, and that is none other than the Lord Jesus Christ. I want you to hear what He has to say in speaking to the Pharisees:

Ye are of your father the devil, and the lusts of your father ye will do. He was a murderer from the beginning, and abode not in the truth, because there is no truth in him. When he speaketh a lie, he speaketh of his own; for he is a liar, and the father of it. (John 8:44)

Our Lord used some very strong language there, I'm sure you'll agree. He said, very definitely and very directly, that the devil is a liar, and not only that but he is the father of lies. I don't know who the mother is, but I can tell you who the father is. We can trace the lie to him. It was an awful thing this creature did, and he is called a liar.

The name that Scripture gives to him is very interesting. I want you to notice it for a moment. In the original Greek it is *diabolos,* and by transliteration we get the word *devil. Diabolos* comes from two words, a preposition *dia* and a verb *bole* that means "to throw." It actually means to throw across. *Diabolos* would mean to say a word here, then to cross over and say something different over there. That's the way it gets the meaning of the lie, you see. That's who Satan is. He says something here but he goes over to the other side and says something else there.

It's quite interesting that our Lord, when He was here, taught in *paraboles,* that is, parables. It's the same verb, *bole,* only a different preposition, *para.* And *para* means to be put by the side of. You put a parable by the side of something to measure it. Someone has well said that a parable is an earthly story with a heavenly meaning. *Paraboles* is "to measure," to get at the truth. But a *diabolos* is something that's thrown across to twist and distort the truth. And the devil is a liar. His very name means "slanderer."

The devil is introduced in Scripture as a liar. The first recorded thing he ever said was a lie. You remember that he came to Eve and, oh, how subtle he was! He didn't come up and contradict God directly, he never has done that. He comes up and says something like this, "Hath God said . . . ?" Well, you know that raises a question. Has He?

You will remember in the case of Job, Satan didn't come before God with the charge, "Job is beating his wife"; nor did he say, "Job is getting drunk every Saturday night." Here's what he said: "Doth Job fear God for nought?" You may scratch your head and say, "Well, I wonder if there's something back of that remark." My friend, hold that in mind when you consider the way this commandment is broken today, and you will see why our

Lord said, "The devil is the father of the lie." Satan is called "the accuser of the brethren," but we are told in 1 John 2:1 that we have an Advocate with the Father, and an advocate means a defender. Why do you and I need an Advocate with the Father? We need one because there's somebody up there accusing us, and the one who is accusing us is none other than Satan, and he's a liar and the father of lies.

Now in Scripture God is put in contrast to the devil. God is truth. Did you ever notice how Scripture emphasizes that? Let me pass on several passages to you—and we're using an abundance of Scripture here as you shall see. This entire message could be given by quoting only Scripture.

In Deuteronomy 32:4, "He is . . . a God of truth and without iniquity, just and right is he." In Numbers 23:19 it says that "God is not a man, that he should lie. . . ." In Isaiah 65:16, He is called "the God of truth," and in 2 Corinthians 1:18 the definition that is given of Him is, "But as God is true, our word toward you was not yea and nay." And so we find that God is set before us in contrast to Satan. God is truth. The devil is a liar.

Notice also that our Lord Jesus, when He came to this earth, came as One who is the truth. You will recall that John put it like this, "And the Word was made flesh, and dwelt among us, [that is, Jesus Christ pitched His tent among us], (and we beheld his glory, the glory as of the only begotten of the Father), full of grace and truth" (John 1:14).

You will recall that it is also said concerning Him, "For the law was given by Moses, but grace and truth came by Jesus Christ" (John 1:17). Then, when He came to the end of His ministry, He could say to His own, "I am the way, the truth, and the life; no man cometh unto the Father, but by me" (John 14:6).

In contrast to God, who is the truth, there is the devil,

whose very name means that he is a slanderer, that he is a liar. And God says in Proverbs 6 that there are seven things He hates. The first one is a proud look, the second is a lying tongue. God says He hates that, He positively *hates* it!

So much for the origination of the lie, which is, of course, false witnessing.

Identification of the Lie

I wonder if we might spend a moment in identifying the lie. In Exodus 20:16 where we are given this commandment, the literal of it is, "Thou shalt not answer against thy neighbor as a witness of falsehood." Dr. Charles Ryrie says, "This commandment refers first of all to false testimony given in a court of justice." It means to come in and present false evidence, and it means that the one who does that is guilty of perjury.

The purpose of our courts is to establish justice, providing a place where a man might take his case, where the truth might be learned and where the judge can get at the facts so that a right decision might be made concerning him. But a false witness defeats the purpose of the courts. People have lost their property, even lost their lives because of a false witness who went into court. This commandment covers this type of situation. "Thou shalt not bear false witness against thy neighbor."

Now may I say to you that this commandment is limited indeed if confined merely to courts of law, because not many of us have been there or probably ever will go into court. But it has a wider view.

Over in Deuteronomy 5 where these commandments are repeated we are told that the literal rendering of verse 20 uses a little different word from the way it is stated in

Exodus: "Thou shalt not answer against thy neighbor as a witness of vanity." The word *vanity* covers a great deal more than what we have in the statement in Exodus. It is more inclusive because there are more ways of bearing false witness than just going into a court of law.

Did you know that there are more words for breaking this commandment than all the other commandments put together? An unprecedented number of words in our English language describe what it means to break this commandment, so great is the ramification of it. Let me give you some of them—lying, mendacity, prevarication, slander, backbiting, defamation, detraction, belittling, censoriousness, gossip, depreciation, derogation, rumor, vilification, aspersion, forgery, mudslinging, falsehood, guile, hypocrisy, insinuation, innuendo, railing, whispering, talebearing, libel, fib, fable, equivocation, disparagement, fabrication, aberration, deceit, trump up, forswear. That's an ugly brood, isn't it! And that's not all of the little chicks that belong to this vulture, my beloved. There are others that could be added to it, but we don't have space to give all of them.

May I say to you that this commandment can be broken in many, many different ways, and I want you to notice some of these.

It is well for us to understand some things that may seem to you like a paradox if not a contradiction. For example, not every untrue statement is a lie, did you know that? Let me illustrate: The boy in school works a problem in arithmetic and he gets the wrong answer. Now that wrong answer is an untrue statement, but it is not a lie. But if that boy turns around and gives that answer to the boy behind him as if it were the truth when he knows it's not, then that answer becomes a lie.

Allow me to go even further and say something that may seem utterly ridiculous. Some true statements are lies. "Oh," you say, "that couldn't be." Yes, it could be. Let me illustrate again with a homely situation. Suppose a good-looking divorcee has recently moved into a little town. She's crossing the street one morning when a car runs into her and she's knocked down. One of the leading businessmen in the city, the banker who is a deacon in the church, sees the accident. He rushes out and picks her up in his arms. The doctor's office is right there on the square, so he carries her in there. But standing on the corner is the town gossip. She rushes to the telephone and calls the man's wife. She says, "I saw something this morning that will shock you. Your husband was holding this new woman who has come to town in his arms!" May I say, that's a true statement but it is a lie to say it like that. This is what I mean by saying that the true statement sometimes is a lie. To twist testimony in court in a similar manner, purposely injuring and incriminating someone, is perjury.

And then may I add another very strange thing. I do not believe the exaggeration of children is really lying. I do not think these little ones ought to be told that they lie when they exaggerate.

A little boy comes rushing into the house and he says, "Mamma, a big lion just ran across the lawn." She says, "Now, Willie, I was looking out the window. That was not a lion, that's a great big old dog." The boy hangs his head and says, "Yes, Mamma, I guess it was." "Well," she says, "I'll have to wash your mouth out with soap for telling a lie." And she takes him into the bathroom, washes his mouth out and says, "Now you go upstairs, and I want you to get down on your knees and ask God to forgive you for telling a lie." So the little fellow goes upstairs, and after a little while he comes down and she says to him, "Did you ask God to forgive you?"

"Yes, Mamma."

"Well, do you think He forgave you?"

"Oh, yes, Mamma. God told me when He first saw the dog He thought it was a lion too."

May I say, friend, that the exaggeration of a child is not necessarily a lie.

But I move on now to that wider area, and I'd like to give a general heading to the things that we're going to talk about—malicious, malignant and malevolent gossip which comes under the purview of this commandment. God's lie detector, the Word of God, lists several of them, and I'd like to put the label of **POISON** on these bottles and put them up on the shelf so that we might not touch them.

The first one that we'll look at is labeled *slander.* Slander is that lie which is invented with the direct intention of damaging a person's reputation. The motives are generally envy, jealousy, hatred, bitterness or revenge. David knew by bitter experience something along this very line, my beloved. Here is what he said:

Deliver me not over unto the will of mine enemies; for false witnesses are risen up against me, and such as breathe out cruelty. (Psalm 27:12)

May I say that this thing known as slander is something that has hurt many people.

It is interesting to note that many of God's children, from the very beginning, have been harmed by slander. A person who would not dare to draw a gun and shoot someone down will lift a knife behind their back and plunge it into their reputation. Did you know that the prophet Jeremiah was all but cursed in his day because of the very fact that slanderers rose up against him? All of the prophets were wrapped in the dark, sulphurous robe of slander. John the Baptist was accused of having a demon. Even the Lord

Jesus Christ was accused of being a glutton, a winebibber, a deceiver, a Samaritan, a traitor, and one possessed of demons.

Paul traveled all the way through the smog of slander. And in the early church the name "Christian" became a synonym for a malefactor for the very simple reason that the Christians were libeled. It was the thing that drove Jerome from Rome. It lifted its awful head against Martin Luther and the Reformers. Savonarola was persecuted, John Wesley and George Whitefield were hounded by it, Moody felt the lash of slander, Billy Sunday knew what it was, and Billy Graham knows what it is today. And there are others in public life who've experienced such attacks. I'm afraid we have had fine men in our police department in Los Angeles who have come to know something about it also, my beloved.

May I say that it has lifted its ugly head against many good and great men in this world—that awful thing that is known as slander. Using it is the lowest level to which any person can stoop.

I rather disagree with these folk who say that women are more guilty of this than men. Some time ago in a women's magazine there was the statement that women can keep a secret just as well as men, but it takes more of them to do it! I disagree with that. I think men can be and are just as vitriolic today in the statements they make. We're told there's a little group that operates almost like a Christian confidential magazine, discrediting good people and starting rumors against them that will do them harm.

It was a pagan poet who wrote this:

> *Who dares think one thing and another tell?*
> *My soul detests them as the gates of hell.*

And it was the poet Virgil who spoke of this awful thing that "lifted itself like a vulture" and covered a city, and sometimes it would destroy a city.

I remember Dr. James McGinley, when I was with him in Atlanta, talking about this thing. He made this statement to the congregation: "You ought not to worry, though, when people lie about you. It would be awful if what they said were true. Just rejoice that what they are telling about you is a lie. You would need to worry if it were the truth."

My beloved, to start false reports like that is the thing that God condemns in Matthew 5:11, when the Lord Jesus says to those who are His own, "Blessed are ye, when men shall revile you, and persecute you, and shall say all manner of evil against you falsely, for my sake." You are indeed blessed at that time.

There also comes under this what can be labeled *whispering* and *talebearing*. Someone has said that some people will believe anything if it's whispered to them. And someone else has said, "You can't believe all you hear, but you can repeat it." It was Moses, in writing the Law, who recorded in Leviticus 19:16, "Thou shalt not go up and down as a talebearer among thy people. . . ." The picture there is really a humorous one. It is the picture of a merchant who comes here and buys a little gossip, then he goes down there and peddles it to someone else—going from house to house, peddling this thing that is not true at all. He is a talebearer.

A great deal is said in the Word of God concerning this. It is malicious and cruel to repeat a story without first checking to see whether it is true or not. Oh, you've heard how a talebearer operates, and notice how close to Satan's method it is. Generally they don't come right out and make a false charge or a vitriolic statement against someone. They start somewhat like this: "It's too bad about So-and-So, isn't it?"

And you say, "Too bad?"

"Don't you know?"

"No, I don't know."

"Well, the least said the better." Oh, brother! They might as well go ahead and write a book after making a statement like that!

And then sometimes it's like this: "Does his wife know?" or "Well, you know why she's popular, don't you?" Isn't it awful to make statements like that? Also there's "Have you heard?" and "Don't quote me," which are used a great deal.

Several years ago I picked up this poem written by Lydell Hillite:

GOSSIP TOWN

Have you ever heard of Gossip Town
  on the shores of Falsehood Bay
Where old Dame Rumor with rustling gown
  is going the livelong day?

It isn't far to Gossip Town
  for people who want to go.
The Idleness Train will take you there
  in just an hour or so.

The Falsehood Road is a popular route,
  and most folks start that way,
But it's a steep downgrade; if you don't look out
  you'll land in Falsehood Bay.

You glide through the Valley of Vicious Folk
  and into the Tunnel of Hate,

Then crossing the Add-to Bridge you'll walk
  right into the City Gate.

The principal street is called "They Say,"
  and "I've Heard" is the public well,
And the breezes that blow from Falsehood
  Bay are laden with "Don't You Tell."

In the midst of the town is Telltale Park—
  you're never quite safe while there,
For its owner is Madame Suspicious Remark
  who lives on the street "Don't Care."

Just back of the Park is Slanderers' Row,
  and 'twas there that Good Name died,
Pierced by a dart from Jealousy Bow
  in the hands of Envious Pride.

From Gossip Town, Peace long since has fled,
  but Trouble, Grief and Woe,
And Sorrow and Care you will meet instead
  if you ever chance to go.

Beloved, I hope you don't go. Actually, to be guilty of
whispering and talebearing you don't have to say a
word—you can merely lift an eyebrow.

The most vicious form of talebearing is to introduce
a rumor in a prayer meeting by requesting prayer for
someone. A young preacher here in Southern California,
when I first came to this area, told me that he had a
prayer meeting in his church that met in the afternoon.
He had to stop it. It had become so popular he wondered
why, and he learned that, if you wanted to find out what
was going on in the neighborhood, that was the place to

go! It started out like this, "Do we have any requests for prayer?" Somebody would get up and say, "Yes, I think we ought to pray for Ms. So-and-So," and somebody would look around and add, "Well, there's a lot of talk going around. As you know, I'm her friend, and I know some of it is true. I think we ought to pray for her." May I say, my beloved, his church was almost wrecked because of that sort of thing being introduced in prayer meetings! My, how we need to watch ourselves in these days in that kind of situation!

I had the privilege once of being with a preacher who had been a target for gossip. Another preacher had started a false rumor about him, and unfortunately, when it came to me, I believed it. Then I found out that this man was doing a wonderful piece of work, and God was blessing him in a remarkable sort of way.

It was David again, in Psalm 140:1–4, who prayed,

Deliver me, O LORD, from the evil man, and preserve me from the violent man who imagines mischiefs in their heart; continually are they gathered together for war.

It sounds as if an enemy is coming against him in warfare, but David was a man of war. He was never afraid of anybody in battle. Here's what he was afraid of:

They have sharpened their tongues like a serpent; adders' poison is under their lips. . . . Keep me, O LORD, from the hands of the wicked. . . .

That was David's prayer for God's protection—and we all need that!

The Epistle of James in a practical manner says that this little member we have right here in our mouths is the most dangerous thing in the world. You can tame everything on the face of the earth, but you can't tame the little tongue. Alcohol today is a great curse in America, probably our greatest curse and maybe our undoing. Alcohol will eventually destroy America if a nuclear attack doesn't do it first. However, I say to you that there's more said in the Word of God about the abuse of the tongue than there is about the abuse of alcohol. I used to say that if you would show me one verse of Scripture for the abuse of alcohol, I'd show you ten verses for the abuse of the tongue. I was wrong. I'll show you fifty verses for every verse you show me about the abuse of alcohol—and that's not in any way condoning alcohol!

But because of the damage done by false witness, it is one of the laws that God puts His finger on, and He says this type of lying is a dangerous, awful thing in this world.

Let me mention other ways in which this commandment is broken. It is broken by flattery. This is the most subtle form of all. I do believe that we need to give recognition to people when they've done a good job. You know we can damn with faint praise, and we can praise with faint damns, but may I say, flattery and back-scratching in Christian circles is a dangerous thing. We need to be real and genuine.

Flattery has destroyed kings in the past. The psalmist says, "Deliver me from the man who flatters with his tongue." And David went on to say concerning this man, "The words of his mouth were smoother than butter, but war was in his heart; his words were softer than oil, yet were they drawn swords" (Psalm 55:21). Flattery is a dangerous weapon.

It destroyed King Ahab (1 Kings 22). Poor Ahab wanted to listen to flattery, and he would tolerate only the men around him who would flatter him. It destroyed him. He listened to the false prophets. And it is said that Louis XIV of France was destroyed because he listened to the men who flattered him instead of listening to good advice.

We need to pray for our President and for anyone who is in a high position. He is sure to be flattered, and when he is flattered he is apt to believe it. That will undermine and destroy him, my beloved. Flattery is a way of breaking this ninth commandment.

Then may I mention another way this commandment is broken, and that is by implication of motives. I knew a man who, when I would do something, would come to me and say, "You did this, didn't you?"

I'd say, "Yes."

"Well, I know you did it for such-and-such a reason!"

"Wait a minute, brother, I did not do it for that reason." But that didn't keep him from going out and saying I had an ulterior motive for doing it. I believe that ascribing a wrong motive to a person's conduct is one of the most dangerous ways of breaking this ninth commandment.

Now let me bring to your attention one more of this filthy brood, and I'll mention it like this: The science of physics has long debated the question, "If a tree falls in the depths of the forest with a great crash and there's no one there who hears it, does it make a sound?" They have debated that pro and con for years. I think the scientific answer is no, and I want to say to you that the biblical answer is no. God says that we are responsible even in listening to a gossiper.

Oh, my friend, do you listen to gossip? Do you hear someone's name blackened in your presence? And do you dare stand there, cowardly, and not lift your voice in defense of that individual? If you were watching a bank being robbed, and the bank robber came by your car, took a bag of money and put it in the backseat saying to you, "It's yours," then you just got in your car and drove off, I'll tell you this, you would be arrested and you would be considered guilty along with the robber. May I say, friend, when you hear something and you pause to listen and do nothing about it, you're as guilty before God as the one who says it. "Thou shalt not bear false witness against thy neighbor."

Destination of the Lie

Finally, let me mention these things that have to do with the destination of the lie. Where is the lie going to end, and the liar? The writer of the Proverbs wrote,

A false witness shall not be unpunished, and he that speaketh lies shall not escape. (Proverbs 19:5)

And God repeats that again in verse 9:

. . . He that speaketh lies shall perish.

And then David could write,

Whoso secretly slandereth his neighbor, him will I cut off. . . . (Psalm 101:5)

When we move to the last book of the Bible, do you want to know what God says is going to come in the future to the one who bears false witness? Referring to the New Jerusalem, the eternal home of the believer, He says,

And there shall in no way enter into it anything that defileth, neither he that worketh abomination, or

maketh a lie; but they who are written in the Lamb's book of life. (Revelation 21:27)

And again John records in the very last chapter in Scripture:

For outside are dogs, and sorcerers, and fornicators, and murderers, and idolaters, and whosoever loveth and maketh a lie. (Revelation 22:15)

That's harsh, I grant you. I can't think of words any more harsh than that, but it's God's warning today, for our Lord says,

But I say unto you that every idle word that men shall speak, they shall give account of it in the day of judgment. (Matthew 12:36)

Somebody's going to say, "Well, Dr. McGee, we're not under the Ten Commandments, and we've heard you say that we're not!" My friend, it is true that we are not under the Ten Commandments as a way of salvation, but I say to you that God wanted to make sure that none of us tried to get out from under this commandment. You will remember that in the early church the first judgment that came upon the Christians was a judgment of death upon two liars. Ananias and Sapphira were struck dead by God because they dared to lie, my beloved, so that it might be a warning to His church.

You and I—even as those believers in the first century—have been called as witnesses. The Lord Jesus said, "Ye shall be witnesses unto Me." And, my friend, if God has called us to be witnesses, we are to be *true* witnesses. If we circulate a false report concerning anyone, who is going to believe us when we say that the grace of God has saved us, my beloved? That's the reason God has put so much in His Word concerning this.

I want to conclude with this little story that Dr. Graebner of Concordia Theological Seminary told. It's about a Lutheran preacher, years ago, in an eastern state where there was a mental institution. This Lutheran preacher was interested in abnormal psychology and attempted to carry on a ministry in this institution. He went out there every week, sometimes two and three times. Of special interest to him was a man there who was always sitting alone in a room, staring out into space. And as he sat there staring, he would keep repeating, "What have I done to these people? What have I done to these people?" The warden there told the preacher the story behind this man. He had been a merchant in a little town, a prosperous, well-to-do merchant. It was a small town, and he was the only one in that particular business. Then some time after he was well established another man came into this little town and opened the same kind of business. In attempting to build up his own trade, the new man started in with a deliberate, definite system of scattering falsehoods concerning his competitor who was respected in the community. He questioned his motives. He made little statements about him to various people about him. He said different things about the prices he had on his merchandise, and before long people began to be suspicious. Because the tendency of human nature is to believe a bad story rather than a good one, people began to wonder. His business fell off and he actually became mentally unbalanced. The poor man became unfriendly to his customers, and it wasn't long until he was bankrupt. He lost everything. He became a mental patient and was brought to this institution.

The warden, who was an agnostic, said this to the

preacher: "If there's a God in heaven, He won't let that other merchant get by with this sort of thing." The preacher assured him that there is a God in heaven and that the man would not get by with it, and certainly not eternally.

And so the years went by. The pastor continued to minister in this institution and one day after many years the warden said to him, "Come here, I have a patient to show you." He took him down the corridor where they put those who were in padded cells, and behind iron bars he showed him the worst mental case he'd ever seen in his life. The warden said, "You remember the man upstairs who sits all day long repeating, 'What have I done to these people?' And I told you about the merchant who had opened up across the street from him and had circulated those false reports and rumors. Well, here is the guilty man." He said, "You know, I've always been an agnostic, but I believe now that there is a God because I know a God in heaven would never let a man get by with what that man did."

This brings us back to the verse of Scripture I used to open this message, "Set a watch, O Lᴏʀᴅ, before my mouth; keep the door of my lips" (Psalm 141:3).

A benediction used so frequently that it may sound trite to us is most appropriate in concluding this message:

Let the words of my mouth, and the meditation of my heart, be acceptable in thy sight, O Lᴏʀᴅ, my strength, and my redeemer. (Psalm 19:14)

My beloved, written in stone with the finger of God is this ninth commandment:

"Tʜᴏᴜ sʜᴀʟᴛ ɴᴏᴛ ʙᴇᴀʀ ꜰᴀʟsᴇ ᴡɪᴛɴᴇss ᴀɢᴀɪɴsᴛ ᴛʜʏ ɴᴇɪɢʜʙᴏʀ."

CHAPTER 10

COVETING—THE SECRET SIN
The Tenth Commandment

Thou shalt not covet thy neighbor's house; thou shalt not covet thy neighbor's wife, nor his manservant, nor his maidservant, nor his ox, nor his ass, nor anything that is thy neighbor's. (Exodus 20:17)

When your neighbor drives up in a new automobile, how do you feel about it? Sometimes we say, "I wish we had the car and they had one just like it." But what we really mean is that we'd rather have that car than see them have it!

The Lord, who knows our hearts better than anybody, prefaced His parable of the rich fool in Luke with this warning:

And he said unto them, Take heed, and beware of covetousness; for a man's life consisteth not in the abundance of the things which he possesseth. (Luke 12:15)

Knowing there would be some question about the meaning of coveting, our Lord was explicit. They were not to covet their neighbor's house, his wife, his property or *anything* that belonged to him.

The command against covetousness shows that it is a sin just to feel an excessive desire for what belongs to another. In our New Testament the word *covet* is usually translated by the words *lust* or *desire* and in some places by *concupiscence*. The basic meaning of covet is "to set the heart on," literally "to pant after."

Since illustrations help us more than definitions in understanding what covetousness is, the Word of God gives many examples of men who were overcome by this secret sin—Laban, Balaam, Achan, Saul, Ahab, Gehazi, Judas, Ananias, Felix, etc.

Achan

We'll start with one of the best known, Achan, who was a member of the army of Israel in their conquest of the Promised Land. It happened when the people of Israel were in the flush of victory. They had overcome Jericho! Although it was God's victory, in a short time Israel thought of it as their victory. And then came the defeat at Ai.

Now notice that the explicit command of God as relayed by Joshua was that nothing was to be salvaged in the city but the silver, gold, and vessels of bronze and iron, which were to be placed in the treasury of the Lord. No soldier was to take anything for himself:

And ye, in every way keep yourselves from the accursed thing, lest ye make yourselves accursed, when ye take of the accursed thing, and make the camp of Israel a curse, and trouble it. (Joshua 6:18)

So after the humiliating and costly defeat at Ai, God told Joshua that Israel had sinned, and it was up to him to find the guilty party. By process of elimination, Achan was found to be the guilty one, and he confessed it.

And Joshua said unto Achan, My son, give, I pray thee, glory to the LORD** God of Israel, and make confession unto him, and tell me now what thou hast done; hide it not from me. And Achan answered Joshua, and said, Indeed I have sinned against the L**ORD** God of Israel, and thus and thus have I done: When I saw among the spoils a beautiful Babylonish garment, and two hundred shekels of silver, and a wedge of gold of fifty shekels weight, then I coveted them, and took them; and, behold, they are hidden in the earth in the midst of my tent, and the silver under it.** (Joshua 7:19–21)

Notice the steps of Achan's sin. He saw, he coveted, he took. These are the steps of the sin of the flesh. Gossip, criticism, envy, and jealousy are all sins of the flesh. They cause strife and trouble. For instance, criticism builds up your ego. It calls attention to yourself. It makes you look better than the person you are criticizing. The old sin of the flesh sees, covets, and then takes.

Now what did Achan do when he was confronted? He confessed. He laid it right out. For believers today, how are we going to overcome the flesh? We have to deal with sin in our lives.

John's first epistle makes clear what we cannot do:

. . . God is light, and in him is no darkness at all. If we say that we have fellowship with him, and walk in darkness, we lie, and do not the truth. (1 John 1:5, 6)

If you say you are having fellowship with God and are living in sin, you are not kidding anybody. You certainly are not having fellowship with Him, and you know it.

Now suppose we deny that we have sinned.

If we say that we have no sin, we deceive ourselves, and the truth is not in us. (1 John 1:8)

But what are we to do?

If we confess our sins, he is faithful and just to forgive us our sins, and to cleanse us from all unrighteousness. (1 John 1:9)

The thing to do is to keep the communication open between you and God. And the only way you can do it is by confessing your sin. John adds,

If we say that we have not sinned, we make him a liar, and his word is not in us. (1 John 1:10)

That's strong language, friend. God says if we say we have no sin we are lying. And I believe He's accurate. But what do we do about it? We are to confess our sins.

How are we to do that? True confession does not deal in generalities. Spell it out as Achan did: "I saw them; I coveted them; I took them." Tell God everything that is in your heart—just open it up to Him. You might as well tell Him because He already knows all about it.

Mel Trotter told about a man on the board of his Pacific Garden Mission, a doctor who, when he prayed, would say, "Lord, if I have sinned, forgive my sins." Mel Trotter got tired of listening to that. Finally he went to the doctor and said to him, "Listen, Doc, you say, 'If I have sinned.' Don't you know whether or not you have sinned?"

The doctor said, "Well, I guess I do."

"Don't you know what your sin is?"

"No."

Mel Trotter said, "If you don't know, then guess at it!"

The next time the doctor prayed, Mel said, he guessed it the first time!

It is amazing, friends, the way we beat around the bush even in our praying. Just go to God and tell Him exactly what your sin is. That is confession. There can be no joy in your life; there can be no power in your life; there can be no victory in your life until there is confession of sin.

> **And Joshua said, Why hast thou troubled us? The LORD shall trouble thee this day. And all Israel stoned him with stones, and burned them with fire, after they had stoned them with stones.** (Joshua 7:25, 26)

This is a serious situation, and it is emphasized for believers in the New Testament:

> **For if ye live after the flesh, ye shall die; but if ye, through the Spirit, do mortify the deeds of the body, ye shall live.** (Romans 8:13)

There are many Christians who are not living. Dwight L. Moody put it in this quaint way: "Some people have just enough religion to make them miserable." There are many miserable saints because they do not deal with the sin in their lives. The apostle Paul said:

> **For if we would judge ourselves, we should not be judged. But when we are judged, we are chastened of the Lord, that we should not be condemned with the world.** (1 Corinthians 11:31, 32)

Ahab's Vineyard

Another of the best-known cases of covetousness is that of Ahab wanting the vineyard of Naboth. Let's take a look at that passage in 1 Kings 21:

And it came to pass after these things, that Naboth, the Jezreelite, had a vineyard, which was in Jezreel, close to the palace of Ahab, king of Samaria. And Ahab spoke unto Naboth, saying, Give me thy vineyard, that I may have it for a garden of herbs, because it is near unto my house, and I will give thee for it a better vineyard than it; or, if it seem good to thee, I will give thee the worth of it in money. And Naboth said to Ahab, The Lord forbid me, that I should give the inheritance of my fathers unto thee. (1 Kings 21:1–3)

A few years ago I was in Samaria, and I must confess that it is one of the most beautiful spots in the land. You can stand on the hill of Samaria where Ahab and Jezebel's palace stood, and you can see Jerusalem to the south, the valley of Esdraelon and the Sea of Galilee to the north, the Jordan River on the east, and the Mediterranean Sea on the west. It has a beautiful view on all four sides. There are not many places like that. If I were living in Israel, that would be the spot where I would like to have my home.

Naboth had a vineyard in this area, and as I stood on that beautiful hill I wondered what side it was on. We do know it was nearby. With as lovely a palace as Ahab had, you would think he would be satisfied. But no, he wanted that vineyard. Naboth did not want to sell it for the very simple reason that the vineyard was his patrimony. It was what God had given his ancestors, and it had been passed down from father to son. But now here is a king who wants it, and it takes a pretty brave man to turn him down.

And Ahab came into his house sullen and displeased because of the word which Naboth, the Jezreelite,

**had spoken to him; for he had said, I will not give
thee the inheritance of my fathers. And he lay down
upon his bed, and turned away his face, and would
eat no food.** (1 Kings 21:4)

Ahab, wicked as he is, is like a spoiled brat and won't
eat now because he cannot have what he wants—he can't
have Naboth's vineyard!

Ahab didn't have any ideas about how to get Naboth's
vineyard, but his wife Jezebel did. She was masculine in
her manner, a dominant and domineering woman. I
would have been afraid of her myself! I can assure you
that she was determined to work out something that
would enable her husband to get it. Notice what happened next.

When he told her why he was pouting she said to him:

**. . . Dost thou now govern the kingdom of Israel?
Arise, and eat food, and let thine heart be merry. I
will give thee the vineyard of Naboth, the Jezreelite.**
(1 Kings 21:7)

She contrived a nice little plot and arranged to have two
lawless men be false witnesses against Naboth. They
said that he blasphemed God and the king. Naboth was
then carried out of the city and stoned to death. Can you
think of anything more unjust than this? Well, it has
happened many times in the history of the world. Often
the man on top who already has too much of everything
has taken advantage of the little man.

Did Ahab get by with it? My friend, you don't get by
with sin. I don't care who you are—the day will come
when you are going to have to settle up. And the day
came when Ahab had to settle up.

And it came to pass, when Jezebel heard that Naboth
was stoned, and was dead, that Jezebel said to Ahab,
Arise, take possession of the vineyard of Naboth, the
Jezreelite, which he refused to give thee for money;
for Naboth is not alive, but dead. And it came to
pass, when Ahab heard that Naboth was dead, that
Ahab rose up to go down to the vineyard of Naboth,
the Jezreelite, to take possession of it. And the word
of the LORD came to Elijah, the Tishbite, saying,
Arise, go down to meet Ahab, king of Israel, who is
in Samaria; behold, he is in the vineyard of Naboth,
where he is gone down to possess it. And thou shalt
speak unto him, saying, Thus saith the LORD, Hast
thou killed, and also taken possession? And thou
shalt speak unto him, saying, Thus saith the LORD,
In the place where dogs licked the blood of Naboth
shall dogs lick thy blood, even thine. (1 Kings 21:15–
19)

And that's not all:

And of Jezebel also spoke the LORD, saying, The dogs
shall eat Jezebel by the wall of Jezreel. (1 Kings
21:23)

When Jezebel came in and announced to Ahab, "Naboth is dead, and you can have the vineyard," it looked
like they had gotten by with this wickedness, didn't it?
No, remember that God has said, "Be not deceived, God
is not mocked: for whatever a man soweth, that shall he
also reap" (Galatians 6:7). If you and I could speak with
men from the past—whether they were God's men or
Satan's—they would tell us that this is an immutable law
of God; it cannot be changed. Both of these judgments
were fulfilled to the letter.

Micah's Lament

God sent the prophet Micah to denounce the covetousness of Israel.

And they covet fields, and take them by violence, and houses, and take them away; so they oppress a man and his house, even a man and his heritage. (Micah 2:2)

So what the heads of government practiced, those down below began to practice. The wealthy began to seize the fields that they coveted because they had the money and the power to do it.

My, how that method is being used in our contemporary society! The little businessman doesn't stand much of a chance for survival in the culture we have produced. The big operators are in control, and they frankly admit that they are in business for the profits. But sometimes the word *profit* is a synonym for *covetousness*. This was the great sin of Israel. And likewise it is the great sin of America.

Even though God had made laws to protect the poor, the rich always found ways to get around them, of course. All through the Scriptures we see that God is on the side of the poor. As Abraham Lincoln used to say, "God must love poor people because He made so many of them." The Lord Jesus Himself experienced the poverty of this earth. And He frequently warned against coveting.

And he said unto them, Take heed, and beware of covetousness; for a man's life consisteth not in the abundance of the things which he possesseth. (Luke 12:15)

And in Hebrews 13:5 the Bible says:

Let your manner of life be without covetousness, and be content with such things as ye have; for he hath said, I will never leave thee, nor forsake thee.

These are certainly good verses for many Christians in this age of crass materialism, when it seems that "things" are so important and occupy so much of our time. Covetousness is one of the outstanding sins of this hour. This is not a sin that others can see you commit, and at times you may not even be aware you are committing it. St. Francis of Assisi once said, "Men have confessed to me every known sin except the sin of covetousness."

The Rich Fool

And he spoke a parable unto them, saying, The ground of a certain rich man brought forth plentifully. And he thought within himself, saying, What shall I do, because I have no place to bestow my crops? And he said, This will I do: I will pull down my barns, and build greater; and there will I bestow all my crops and my goods. And I will say to my soul, Soul, thou hast much goods laid up for many years; take thine ease. Eat, drink, and be merry. (Luke 12:16–19)

Notice the rich man's emphasis on himself in this passage: "What shall *I* do, because *I* have no place to bestow *my* crops?" Notice again what he decided to do.

And he said, This will I do: I will pull down my barns, and build greater; and there will I bestow all my crops and my goods. And I will say to my soul, Soul, thou hast much goods laid up for many years; take thine ease. Eat, drink, and be merry. But God said unto him, Thou fool, this night thy soul shall be required of thee; then whose shall those things be, which thou hast provided? (Luke 12:18–20)

This man had gathered all of his treasure on earth but had stored none in heaven. The same idea is expressed in this epitaph:

> *Here lies John Racket*
> *In his wooden jacket.*
> *He kept neither horses nor mules.*
> *He lived like a hog.*
> *He died like a dog.*
> *And left all his money to fools.*

Our Lord called the man in this parable a fool, but notice what kind of man he probably was. All outward appearances indicate that he was a good man by the world's standards, a law-abiding citizen, a good neighbor, a fine, family man. He was above suspicion, living the good life in suburbia in the best residential area of the city. He was not a wicked man or a member of the Mafia. He was not in crooked politics. He was not an alcoholic or keeping a woman on the side. This man seems to be all right. Yet our Lord called him a fool. Why? This man thought only of himself, and he was covetous.

This is the way many people live. The parable of the rich fool is one of the most pungent paragraphs in the Word of God. The philosophy of the world today is, "Eat, drink and be merry, for tomorrow we die." Our Lord said, "That's the problem, that's what makes a man a fool." If you live as though this life is all there is, if you live just for self and as though there is nothing beyond death, you are a fool.

And he said unto his disciples, Therefore, I say unto you, Be not anxious for your life, what ye shall eat; neither for the body, what ye shall put on. The life is more than food, and the body is more than raiment. Consider the ravens; for they neither sow nor reap, which neither have storehouse nor barn, and God feedeth them; how much more are ye better than the fowls? (Luke 12: 22-24)

Now of course it is not wrong to store up things. The problem with the rich fool was covetousness. He was trying to get more and more and more. That is the curse of godless capitalism. Have you noticed the strong judgment that is pronounced upon the rich in the last days? James 5:1 describes it: "Come now, ye rich men, weep and howl for your miseries that shall come upon you." Riches have become a curse. Notice what the Scripture says in 1 Timothy 6:6, 8 and 9

But godliness with contentment is great gain. . . . And having food and raiment let us be therewith content. But they that will be rich fall into temptation and a snare, and into many foolish and hurtful lusts, which drown men in destruction and perdition.

Our great nation thought that the almighty dollar would solve the problems of the world, but we are in a bigger mess than ever. We should search our hearts and ask ourselves, "Am I living for this life only?" Our Lord said, "Go look at the birds, and learn something from them."

And he said, That which cometh out of the man, that defileth the man. For from within, out of the heart of men, proceed evil thoughts, adulteries, fornications, murders, thefts, covetousness, wickedness, deceit, lasciviousness, an evil eye, blasphemy, pride, foolishness. All these evil things come from within, and defile the man. (Mark 7:20–23)

I'll guarantee you that if you will buy the morning paper wherever you live and will read it through, you will find that this is what came out during the last twenty-four hours. These all come out of the heart of man, and that is why the Lord Jesus says, "Ye must be born again."

From the Pen of the Apostle Paul

"Thou shalt not covet" is the one commandment that gave the apostle Paul a lot of trouble. Notice what he says in Romans 7:7, 8:

What shall we say then? Is the law sin? God forbid. Nay, I had not known sin but by the law; for I had not known coveting, except the law had said, Thou shalt not covet. But sin, taking occasion by the commandment, wrought in me all manner of coveting. For apart from the law sin is dead.

Paul could go down through nine of those commandments and say, "I keep those commandments." Can you say that today? I don't believe there's a person reading this who can say, "I keep all ten of the commandments, I've never broken any of the Ten Commandments."

What Paul's saying is, "Though I can take the first nine and say that I keep those, when I come to the tenth commandment, it's the one that slays me."

In this portion of Romans 7, Paul becomes very personal. He uses the pronoun "I" over thirty times from verse 7 through verse 25. Paul speaks of "I . . . I . . . I." Now sometimes it becomes extremely boring when a person just talks about himself, but there are times when a testimony is a very good thing. And this is a testimony of defeat, not a testimony of victory. However, it does lead to victory, as we shall see.

Now Paul faces up to his failure. Instead of going to a psychiatrist, he crawls upon God's couch and lays his soul bare. I believe God permitted it so that you and I might learn a great lesson from this man's experience.

No Victory in the Law

Paul thought that when he was saved he would live the Christian life by the Law, but he found that the Mosaic Law did not give him victory. The fact of the matter is, Paul puts the Law down as almost tantamount to sin, because he says what the Law did for him was just lead him to sin. So now he has to answer the question, "Is the Law sin?" And he answers it here in Romans 7:7 and 8. I'll give you my translation: "What shall we say then, is the law sin? Away with the thought! On the contrary, I should not have known or have been conscious of sin except through the law, for I had not known illicit desire [that is, coveting], but sin, getting a start through the commandment, produced [or wrought out] in me all manner of illicit desire, for apart from the law, sin is dead."

The picture here is this: Paul says that he took the Ten Commandments out of the Law and put them down on his life, and when he did he found out he could get through nine of those commandments unscathed and be able to say, "Well, I kept these." Before Paul knew it was wrong to covet, there was no conviction of sin. But now the Law reveals what is sin. Sin was dormant until the Law was given. Now Paul says, "But the tenth commandment slew me," because it says, "Thou shalt not covet," and Paul says, "I coveted."

Coveting Is the Secret Sin

Coveting is a sin that can't be discerned very easily. A person can covet and not be discovered. If you steal, you'll be found out, believe me. If you steal, you're going to leave fingerprints, or you're going to have the goods in your hands, so you'll be found out eventually. If you murder, you have a corpus delicti, and if you commit adultery, there's one thing for sure, somebody else knows about it! So that you don't always get by with sin in breaking these other commandments, but this commandment, "Thou shalt not covet"—oh, my friend, you can sit in church and covet and nobody will be the wiser. You can even stand in the pulpit and covet. You see, the Law revealed that this was wrong, and that was the only way in the world Paul had of finding out it was wrong. The Law says, "Thou shalt not covet." That's the way he found out about it. The Law really shows us up.

Our contemporary society also says that sort of thing, that when you break a civil law, ignorance will not help you at all. God has put up laws, you see, and Paul says,

"Before I knew about that commandment of coveting, why, I could covet without feeling guilty."

But then Paul says, "When that law came to me and I found out that God says, 'Thou shalt not covet,' it wrought in me all manner of illicit desire, for apart from the law, sin is dead." You see, it doesn't stand out as transgression at all. Isn't it interesting that our human nature is so made that when we find out a thing is wrong, then we want to do it—especially when *God* says we are not to do it.

Why is it today that a great many people take particular delight in defying God? Well, it's natural. You and I have a nature that's in rebellion against God. Whether you and I will admit it or not, we have a nature that hates God. It is in rebellion against Him, won't be obedient to Him. And, friend, you and I have that old nature today—it's human nature. It is constantly pulling us down, and this is the nature that God gave the Law to curb. The purpose of the Law is to try to control the old nature.

I've heard several men mention this. One man was telling me some time ago, "Before I was converted, I thought I lived a fairly good life, but now that I've become a Christian I sometimes want to do some of the meanest things!" Do you know what it is? It's that old nature he has—just like the one you and I have. It is in rebellion against God, and will be until we are willing to do what Paul did.

Now for you today it may not be coveting, it may be some other sin. But it's the weakness of your flesh, where that old nature wants to assert itself. Until you are willing to acknowledge it I don't believe there's any deliverance for you—not as long as you are willing to gloss it over, put a little shellac on it, and cover it up. My friend, you had better recognize it. Nail that thing down and deal with it specifically before God. Let me emphasize again 1 John 1:9:

If we confess our sins, he is faithful and just to forgive us our sins, and to cleanse us from all unrighteousness.

And I do not believe that means to go to God and say in a wholesale sort of way, "Lord, I have sinned," and then let it go at that. You call it by name. When you are ordering from a catalog, you don't just tell them, "Send me a bunch of goods; send me some supplies." You list specifically what it is you want. You give the catalog number, you give the page in the catalog, you give the description of the article. You label it!

When you go to God in confession, give Him the catalog number; that is, tell God what it is—He has given these commandments. Tell Him what is in your heart and life. I believe if we'll first of all deal with these things and clean out the old closet and get rid of the skeletons, then we're going to get on good, solid ground to begin to live for God.

May I say, the Law is what revealed to Paul the exceeding sinfulness of sin. You see, the Law was an X ray that was put down on his heart and on his life, and it laid bare the thoughts and intents of his heart. It uncovered the weakness and the ugliness of the sin that was there. So Paul cried out;

Oh, wretched man that I am! Who shall deliver me from the body of this death? (Romans 7:24)

This is not an unsaved man who is crying, "Oh, wretched man that I am!" This is a saved man. The word *wretched* carries with it the note of exhaustion because of the struggle. "Who is going to deliver me?" He is helpless. His shoulders are pinned to the floor—he has been wrestled down. Like old Jacob, he has been crippled. He is calling for help from the outside.

I thank God through Jesus Christ, our Lord. So, then, with the mind I myself serve the law of God; but with the flesh the law of sin. (Romans 7:25)

"I thank God [who gives deliverance] through Jesus Christ, our Lord." This is the answer to Paul's SOS. God has provided deliverance. Both salvation and sanctification come through Christ; He has provided everything we need.

> *Run, run and do, the Law commands*
> *But gives me neither feet nor hands.*
> *Better news the Gospel brings,*
> *It bids me fly and gives me wings.*

CHAPTER 11

THE GREATEST
COMMANDMENT

Then one of them, who was a lawyer, asked him a question, testing him, and saying, Master, which is the great commandment in the law? Jesus said unto him, Thou shalt love the Lord, thy God, with all thy heart, and with all thy soul, and with all thy mind. This is the first and great commandment. And the second is like it, Thou shalt love thy neighbor as thyself. On these two commandments hang all the law and the prophets. (Matthew 22:35-40)

This was the last question put to Christ by His enemies, the religious rulers, when they asked Him which was the greatest commandment. We are told that after He answered this question, they never came to Him again with another question.

While this is the first time our Lord answered the question like this, it is not the first time He made this declaration. This momentous thesis was declared before by our Lord when another lawyer came to Him, testing Him concerning the greatest commandment. It was at that time that our Lord gave to him the wonderful parable of the Good Samaritan:

And, behold, a certain lawyer stood up, and tested him, saying, Master, what shall I do to inherit eternal life? He said unto him, What is written in the law? How readest thou? And he, answering, said,

Thou shalt love the Lord thy God with all thy heart, and with all thy soul, and with all thy strength, and with all thy mind; and thy neighbor as thyself. (Luke 10:25–27)

Apparently there was a feeling among the religious rulers of the day that this was the greatest commandment.

And he [Jesus] said unto him, Thou hast answered right; this do, and thou shalt live. (Luke 10:28)

So our Lord, during His entire ministry, had set before them the fact that this was the greatest commandment.

Now there are two facts of great consequence in the answer that our Lord gave, which are self-evident here. The first one is that Christ did not go to the Ten Commandments to get the greatest commandment. Rather, He went to the passage in Deuteronomy 6:4, 5 where we find the greatest doctrinal statement in the entire Old Testament:

Hear, O Israel: The LORD our God is one LORD: and thou shalt love the LORD thy God with all thine heart, and with all thy soul, and with all thy might.

Now this is the commandment that our Lord said was the greatest. Why didn't He go to the Ten Commandments? He might have taken the first commandment, "Thou shalt have no other gods before me," but He didn't go there. And there are a great many people today who think that He should have taken the commandment of the Sabbath day and made it the greatest, but He didn't do that. The interesting thing is that He went to the Book of Deuteronomy and lifted out a commandment that is not even connected with the Ten Commandments at all. And it is quite interesting that our Lord seemed to have quoted from Deuteronomy more than from any other book in the Scriptures. It was the Book He quoted from twice in the three answers He gave to Satan during His temptation, as recorded in Matthew 4:1-11. And it is also interesting that this is the first Book of the Bible ever to be attacked by the higher critics. The Graf-Wellhausen hypothesis struck at Deuteronomy. It didn't strike at Daniel or another Book of the Bible, but its onslaught was against Deuteronomy. You can see Satan's hatred of this Book, the Book to which our Lord turned to rebuke Satan. Since our Lord Jesus gave a great deal of importance to Deuteronomy, I believe we should be giving it a great deal more attention than we do today—in spite of the fact that it is not very interesting reading.

Our Lord went to Deuteronomy, which was given at the end of the wilderness march. He didn't quote from that which was at the beginning but from that which was at the end. And in the Book of Deuteronomy, you find that the Law had been tested in the crucible of forty years of experience in the wilderness, and it is poured out of the test tube of this rugged experience. Now our Lord comes up with His answer to the question by saying that here is the greatest commandment: "Thou shalt love the LORD thy God with all thy heart, and with all thy soul, and with all thy mind."

There is another thing we should notice which is introductory. On both occasions when Christ spoke of the greatest commandment, He didn't stop with only one; He spoke of two, and He always put these together. First, "Thou shalt love the Lord thy God," and then second, "Thou shalt love thy neighbor as thyself." So here are the first and second commandments which our Lord gave in the order of their importance. And, as you'll find in 1 John, our relationships today are like a triangle. God is at the top, you are on one side, and on the other side is your neighbor. It is a love relationship with God and a love relationship with God's children who are around about you. First John makes it clear that Christ was talking about God's children.

Love in the Old Testament

Now the love for God and the love for the neighbor are both found in the Book of Deuteronomy. This book is not a repetition of Exodus or Leviticus. It does not merely state the Law a second time. In Exodus and Leviticus, you have the emphasis on the Law. But in the Book of Deuteronomy, the emphasis is on love. It may seem strange that the emphasis there is upon love, but the strangest thing of all is that it took God a long time to tell anybody that He loved them. In reading through Genesis, you won't find Him telling anybody He loves them. Neither will you find it in Exodus. In Leviticus and Numbers, He still doesn't tell anybody He loves them.

However, the Book of Deuteronomy is the book that came out after the wilderness experience, when a new generation is entering the land. God says to this new generation, "I want you to know something if you haven't discovered it so far—I *love* mankind!" He had demonstrated it, but He had not said it before. In Deuteronomy 4:37, you will find one of the most wonderful statements:

And because he loved thy fathers, therefore he chose their seed after them, and brought thee out in his sight with his mighty power out of Egypt.

My beloved, that is a glorious, wonderful truth. At the end of the wilderness journey, after they had endured many rugged experiences, there might have been a question in the mind of some of the new generation, *Does God really love us?* They had heard their parents say again and again, "We just don't believe that God really wants to bring us into the land. We don't believe He is interested in us." Now God says to the new generation, "Look back, look back upon your fathers and see how I dealt with them. I loved them. My love for them explains the reason I dealt with them as I did, and you will see that My mercy was extended to them again and again. It was an evidence of My love for them."

In Exodus and Leviticus, you will find that the emphasis is on Law, but even in that there is the mercy and love of God. In Exodus 20:6, which is in the Ten Commandments, we read,

And showing mercy unto thousands of them that love me, and keep my commandments.

And in Leviticus 19:18 we read,

Thou shalt not avenge, nor bear any grudge against the children of thy people, but thou shalt love thy neighbor as thyself: I am the Lord.

You see love in Exodus and Leviticus in a minor note, but it becomes a major note when you get to the Book of Deuteronomy, where we find a law for love: "Thou shalt love the Lord thy God with all thine heart, and with all thy soul, and with all thy might" (6:5). And in the seventh chapter, we find it again:

The Lord did not set his love upon you, nor choose you, because ye were more in number than any peo-

ple; for ye were the fewest of all people. But because the LORD loved you. . . . (v. 7,8)

And when God started telling them how much He loved them, He couldn't let up. He just kept on telling them that He loved them.

May I say that God's love for us is the wonder of wonders, something that we take for granted today, but it was glorious truth in that day. Therefore you find in the Book of Deuteronomy the great principle of the gospel set down for us, "For God so loved the world." In Deuteronomy God says, "I have done this for you because I loved you." And now God says to the world today, "For God so loved the world, that he gave his only begotten Son, that whosoever believeth in him should not perish, but have everlasting life" (John 3:16).

Now today, all conservative groups start off in harmony. But the trouble is that they don't finish in harmony. Both those who are called "covenant theologians" and those who are "dispensational theologians" agree that there is a bifurcation between law and grace. Both groups make a correct division and distinction at this point.

For the law was given by Moses, but grace and truth came by Jesus Christ. (John 1:17)

But I want you to notice something that I feel neither group is emphasizing as they should—and I recognize that I have not always emphasized it, but this message gives us that opportunity. The Lord Jesus Christ came to fulfill the Law, not to destroy it. He made that very clear in Matthew 5:17,

Think not that I am come to destroy the law, or the prophets; I am not come to destroy, but to fulfill.

Now will you notice how He did that. In His life, He kept all the Commandments. He kept the Law, and up to today He is the only person who has ever lived who actually has kept the Commandments—unless you think that you have kept them, and I may be wrong but I don't think you have. No other person has ever kept them. Only of Christ has God been able to say, "This is my beloved Son, in whom I am well pleased" (Matthew 3:17). He hasn't said that about me, and He hasn't said it about you, but He did say it about Christ. In His life, the Lord Jesus kept all the commandments of God and that which expresses the will of God. In His death He kept the ordinances and the testimonies and the sacrifices. He fulfilled the Law in all of its departments, in its many ramifications. In its minutest details, our Lord kept the Law.

Now the great principle of law is love. I think we forget that today. We like to think of the Old Testament as being a little harsh and that God in the Old Testament is a little severe. He is not. He is the God of love, the God of love in the Old Testament as well as the God of law. The great principle of law is always love.

God didn't give law to hurt mankind. "His commandments," the apostle says, "are not burdensome" (1 John 5:3). God's laws are not made by dumbbells in the legislature. These come from God, and they are for the weal and welfare of mankind.

Now God gives us His great principle of the Mosaic Law, which is love, and we express our love by obedience. It must always be so. Will you notice what He says in Deuteronomy 7:9:

Know, therefore, that the LORD thy God, he is God, the faithful God, who keepeth covenant and mercy with them who love him and keep his commandments to a thousand generations.

Now the great principle of the gospel is expressed here in Deuteronomy, and it is expressed in love.

And again will you notice these expressions, beginning with Deuteronomy 4:37:

And because he loved thy fathers, therefore he chose their seed after them, and brought thee out in his sight with his mighty power out of Egypt.

God did that because of love. And here in chapter 6, verse 5:

And thou shalt love the LORD thy God with all thine heart, and with all thy soul, and with all thy might.

And then you will find that Paul mentions this great principle in the Epistle to the Galatians,

For all the law is fulfilled in one word, even in this: Thou shalt love thy neighbor as thyself. (5:14)

Now having made a statement like this, someone asks, "How then is the gospel new if we define the principle of it as being back under law? If you have love in the Old Testament, what's new about love in the New Testament?" Therefore, I want to deal with that particular problem.

Love Extended

Will you notice this, and follow it very carefully: first of all, the love of God has been translated into history by the Incarnation—the birth, the death and the resurrection of Christ—so that Paul could write in Romans 5:8,

But God commendeth his love toward us in that, while we were yet sinners, Christ died for us.

That is the way God reveals His love today, and there is a vast difference. It is one thing to express love by bringing the people of Israel out of Egypt, and it's another thing to die for mankind. It is one thing to come down to the top of Mount Sinai and give commandments; it is quite another thing to come on down and take upon Himself human flesh in order to suffer with mankind, to bleed and to die. That is *love,* my beloved!

May I say that long after the giving of the Law, in the present hour in which we live, God has already extended and revealed His love to us as He never did in the Old Testament. So today salvation is a love story. It is not a cold-blooded business transaction—Jesus shed His blood, cash on the barrelhead. He did shed His blood, but *why* did He do it? He did it because He loved us. Salvation is a love affair.

One of the last books written in the New Testament was the First Epistle of John. Here the apostle John gathers all this together and says, "We love him, because he first loved us" (4:19). Now that is salvation—we love Him because He first loved us. And John makes clear what he means when he says He loved us:

Herein is love, not that we loved God, but that he loved us, and sent his Son to be the propitiation for our sins. (1 John 4:10)

He gave His Son to *die* for us! The cross is the place God manifested His love. And because He did that, we are to love Him.

May I say, there is a grand canyon between the Law and where you stand today. You have the principle of the gospel in Deuteronomy, but you don't actually have the gospel. It is not until you come to the One who left heaven's glory, came to this earth and demonstrated it. It is an historic fact that Jesus died, He was buried, He rose again the third day. That is how God extended and expressed His love to mankind.

Love Defined

Love for God in the Old Testament is not definitive. It was expressed only in obedience. God says to the children of Israel, "If you love Me you will obey Me." Now when we come to the New Testament it is spelled out for us. What do we mean by love? In John 13:34, 35 we are given an adequate and fully delineated definition of love by our Lord:

A new commandment I give unto you, that ye love one another. . . .

I suppose Simon Peter, if the Lord had stopped there, could have said, "That's old stuff—we read that in Deuteronomy." But our Lord kept on going:

As I have loved you, that ye also love one another.

That's the standard of love; that's the norm today, the badge and fraternity pin of those who are His own. The kind of love that He had for us is the love that the believer is to manifest, and anything short of that is not Christian love. It may be something else, but it is not Christian love.

And He went on to say,

By this shall all men know that ye are my disciples, if ye have love one to another.

I wish Christ had said that if I'm a premillennialist and a pretribulationist everybody would know I'm His, but He didn't say that. He said, "If you don't manifest it in love, nobody will know that you belong to Me." Will you read that again? Our Lord said, in John 15:12,

This is my commandment, that ye love one another, as I have loved you.

God does not save you today by your keeping any of His commandments, and the reason is He now has a much higher standard than the Ten Commandments, and He never saves anyone based on what that person does. He saves the one who believes that *God* has done something—that God Himself has paid the penalty for his sins. Then He will save that person. And after He saves him, He says, "Now I want to talk to you about what you are to do." If you are not a Christian, He is not talking to you at this point. But to the believer God says, "Now if you belong to Me, this is My commandment, that you love one another as I have loved you." And if you miss it in verse 12, He repeats it again and again—verse 10: "If ye keep my commandments, ye shall abide in my love, even as I have kept my Father's commandments, and abide in his love." Verse 14: "Ye are my friends, if ye do whatever I command you." Verse 17: "These things I command you, that ye love one another." Now that's spelling it out, is it not? And, as far as the New Testament is concerned, that doesn't end it.

Turning to 1 Corinthians 13, we find the finest statement on love that has ever been penned, and this is from a very fine translation, the *Amplified New Testament:*

> **If I [can] speak in the tongues of men and [even] of angels, but have not love . . . I am only a noisy gong or a clanging cymbal. And if I have prophetic powers—that is, the gift of interpreting the divine will and purpose; and understand all the secret truths and mysteries and possess all knowledge, and if I have [sufficient] faith so that I can remove mountains, but have not love [God's love in me] I am nothing—a useless nobody.** (vv. 1, 2)

The word "love" here is *agape* in the Greek. There are three Greek words that are translated by our English word *love*. One is *eros*, which is never found in the New Testament. We get our word "erotic" from it. If you want the best translation, it is the English word *sex*. That is what the Greeks meant when they used the word *eros*. I do not think it should even be translated by our word "love." The New Testament never uses it. Then there is the word *phileo*, which means "friendship." Now I know there are Greek scholars today who will not make a distinction between *phileo* and *agape*, but the New Testament makes the distinction between *phileo*, which means friendship, and *agape*, which is love as only God can give it.

Now *agape* is the word in 1 Corinthians 13. I'm not going to take the space to go into all of the ramifications here, but this is the most marvelous definition of what love really is. And if you want to know whether you are manifesting love, read 1 Corinthians 13, and may I suggest you use the *Amplified New Testament.*

> **Love endures long and is patient and kind; love never is envious nor boils over with jealousy; is not boastful or vainglorious, does not display itself haughtily. It is not conceited—arrogant and inflated with pride; it is not rude [unmannerly], and does not act unbecomingly. Love . . . does not insist on its own rights or its own way . . . Love never fails—never fades out or becomes obsolete or comes to an end. . . .** (vv. 4, 5, 8)

Paul concludes by saying,

> **And so faith, hope, love abide . . . but the greatest of these is love.** (v. 13)

The greatest of these is love. Faith looks to the past, hope looks to the future, but love is for the present and it is for eternity.

May I say that the thing which is going to characterize heaven is love. It is what Paul meant when he said in Galatians 6:2, "Bear ye one another's burdens, and so fulfill the law of Christ."

Love, if you please, is not defined in the Old Testament, but it is spelled out for us in the New Testament by the Incarnation of the Son of God. It is the love that He had when He left heaven's glory and came to this earth. And anything short of that is not Christian love. It may be mistaken for fellowship. I have had the privilege of speaking at many Rotary Clubs where they emphasize fellowship, and that's good. But unfortunately a great many people in the church think fellowship is all that Christian love is—just a pat on the back. My friend, that is not Christian love. This is a tremendous thing our Lord is saying!

Love Empowered

We come now to the third way in which love was a new commandment. There was no power to express and realize the love of God in the Old Testament. None whatever. As best I can tell, God said, "This is it, I've put it on the line. You either do it or you don't do it. And if you don't do it, I'll punish you. If you do it, I'll bless you." Well, they didn't do it. And the consequences? Look at the history of the Jewish people for the past 3,000 years. An example is their treatment by Hitler, who had some six million Jews killed. But if they could have kept God's Law, not one hand would ever have been put on them. They are a witness to the world that you cannot please God by doing something. They tried it, and they had ideal conditions for it—which we don't have.

God today is saying to mankind, "You have not met My standard, but I am prepared to reach down and lift you up." That is the reason He sent Christ into the world. And now He says that those who have come to Him and are really born-again children of God are to express that same kind of love. He also says, "I'll give you the power for it today—the fruit of the Spirit is love." Now after that, there are other fruits that apparently stem from love, because the language, the grammar, is quite exact. The fruit of the Spirit is not *our* love, joy, peace, et cetera, but it is His love working through us. The one fruit is love, and out of love comes "joy, peace, longsuffering, gentleness, goodness, faith, meekness, self-control . . ."

(Galatians 5:22,23). This is what is produced, not by our own effort but by the Holy Spirit in the life of the believer.

God says the child of God cannot measure up to His standard at all. It is beyond human ability and effort. The Holy Spirit was not given in the Old Testament to enable them to realize the ideal that was expressed in the Law. Today it is expressed by the Holy Spirit indwelling the believer. Paul could say in Romans 7:18, ". . . To will is present with me, but how to perform that which is good I find not." In other words, Paul is saying, "I have a new nature and I want to please Him, I want to love God with all my heart, my soul, my mind, but I fail. I want to love others, but I don't. The will is present with me, but how to perform it, I find not." Then that man who was so defeated in chapter 7 of Romans says in chapter 8 that what he couldn't do through the flesh, the Holy Spirit has now been able to do. And you'll find him writing to the Philippians at the end of his life, "I can do all things through Christ, who strengtheneth me" (4:13). So today God has given a power to believers that enables them to realize this ideal.

I want to conclude with this application. There is a crisis today in evangelical circles. We have spent so much time in trying to remove the mote from the eye of everyone else, we've forgotten the beam in our own eye. We have majored in anti-this and anti-that and anti-something else until today we are all anti's. We don't seem to be pro-anything. Our forte today is to be against anything. The American Association for the Advancement of Atheism went out of business because theological liberalism had put agnostics into the pulpit, and the head of the Four A's said he disbanded his organization because the pulpit was doing his job much better than he was! But evangelicals seem to have their own Four A's today—The American Association Against Anything!

We today declare our historic doctrine of the faith in clear and clarion tones, and we should, but are we manifesting before the world the love that our Lord commanded? We are vocal about our high calling, but there is a lack of conviction and courage for that which is right. *Almost* we are adopting the liberal's definition of love, which is the sloppiest thing you have ever heard. It just slops over on every side with talk about loving everybody—"love, love, love," and what that means is, be a weak sissy.

May I say that we need a strong love, the kind our Lord had when He could denounce the Pharisees and say to them, "You are hypocrites," but then go to the cross and say, "Father, forgive them." And they were forgiven for the crucifixion of the Son of God, otherwise that would have been an unpardonable sin. Afterward many of them were converted, including Saul of Tarsus, who apparently was present at the Crucifixion.

But today the country club exhibits more courtesy than the community church. The bridge club has less gossip than the Bible class. Present-day churches have more doctrine and less love, more turmoil and less theology.

I remember hearing Homer Rodeheaver tell this story many years ago. He said that in a little town back in Arkansas a man drove in to a filling station up on a hill right at the edge of town. It was a Sunday morning about eleven o'clock. When the driver got out of his car, he could hear church bells ringing. He began to look over the town and counted seventeen steeples there. As the manager began to fill up the car with gas, his customer looked around and said, "My, everybody in this town must love God!" The manager, an agnostic, said, "I don't know about that, but I do know this: they *hate* each other." Homer Rodeheaver concluded by saying that the last he heard, that manager was still an agnostic. Of course he was!

My beloved, our churches today need something to go with their doctrine: "By this shall all men know that ye are my disciples, if ye have love one to another" (John 13:35).

A story I have told many times is of Mr. and Mrs. Whittemore, a very respectable, well-to-do couple. They were entertaining house guests, and to give them a novel experience one evening they went slumming and ended up at Jerry McAuley's mission. But that night Mr. and Mrs. Whittemore responded to the invitation to receive Christ and knelt at the altar—she in ermine beside the bums. Later Mrs. Whittemore said, "Since I was saved down here in the slums, I want to do something down here. We never heard the gospel in the society church we attended, and we never were told we were sinners. But Jerry McAuley told us we were sinners and we needed Christ as Savior."

So she started a home for wayward girls. One night several of her girls picked up a young woman who had been pitched out of a basement room. The last man had beaten her and thrown her out in the snow. She was a sorry-looking mess when Mrs. Whittemore took her into that home and nursed her back to health and strength. But that girl was as hard as nails. The day came when the girl was well and ready to leave the home, and Mrs. Whittemore sat down on her bed for the last time, very discouraged. She said, "Rose, I have tried to present to you the gospel that you might be saved as I was saved, but you won't believe." Then Mrs. Whittemore began to cry, and, like a woman, she just put her arm around this girl and hugged her. All of a sudden she discovered that the girl was sobbing. It was the first time she had cried in ten years. She was hard! As Rose cried, Mrs. Whittemore felt that now her heart was open, and it was. She was able to lead her to Christ. It is on record that this girl led 1,700 other girls like herself to Christ before she died several years later.

Do you know what is wrong with evangelical Christianity today? It is not their doctrine, that part is right. What is missing? "By this shall all men know that you are My disciples, if you have *love* one for another."